The Lover's
COMPANION

Edited by
Elizabeth Jane Howard

The Lover's

COMPANION

2924666
8088

David & Charles
Newton Abbot London Vancouver

British Library Cataloguing in Publication Data
The lovers' companion.
  1. Love – Literary collections
  I. Howard, Elizabeth Jane
  808.8'0354   PN6071.L7
ISBN 0-7153-7432-X

Arrangement and introductions
© Elizabeth Jane Howard 1978

Typeset by HBM Typesetting Limited
Standish Street Chorley Lancashire
and printed in Great Britain
by Biddles Limited Guildford
for David & Charles (Publishers) Limited
Brunel House Newton Abbot Devon

Published in Canada
by Douglas David & Charles Limited
1875 Welsh Street North Vancouver BC

CONTENTS

Detailed contents are listed after the introduction to each Part.

For Robin and Mary Howard

INTRODUCTION

Anybody presented with the opportunity of compiling an anthology has really only two problems: knowing what they like (this kind of anthology has nothing of history or the monograph about it—personal taste is all), and deciding what methods of arrangement will be most likely to win readers to their choice. The first problem isn't too difficult; I hope I don't yet know *all* that I shall like for the rest of my life, but there has certainly been no shortage of material; indeed, some of the omissions will be squeaking and gibbering in the back-streets of my mind for a long time. The second problem is more serious; it can be quite enjoyable disagreeing with another person's taste: it can be very irritating to find their methods of presenting works either confusing or monotonous. I have opted for a chronology of love rather than an historical chronology of the writers concerned. This is not only to avoid blocks of writing in—say—the fashion of the early nineteenth century, but also to juxtapose very different people in the same mood of love. I have divided the book into five parts and each part has its own introduction.

I have confined myself to heterosexual love only because the subject is such a vast one that some restrictions were necessary. In one or two cases—notably Shakespeare's sonnets—this ruling may seem ambiguous: there I have included only those sonnets where the sex of the recipient is unimportant. The excerpts consist of poems, letters, scenes from plays and novels, pieces of autobiography, and remarks of a general nature. In the cases of the plays and novels I have provided the briefest possible run-ups to the situations quoted.

Many readers will find much of the time that they also know what I like: I have never omitted anything simply because it is well known: many works, notably poetic works are generally read and regarded as good because they *are* good, and this is not meant to be a collection of needles in the haystack of my taste.

I should like to thank my cousin, Jean MacGibbon, for some useful and interesting contributions, and my husband, Kingsley Amis, for his advice, notably about the poetry, and for much general patient and informed support.

Part I

FIRST LOVE, FIRST MEETINGS

I had thought, when I embarked upon this part, that there would be an enormous range of choice, and, indeed, there are a number of pieces elsewhere in this book that might have been put here, as first love can also involve instant courtship, or, at the very least, a declaration of some kind. Sometimes it can be a one-sided affair; Turgenev's *First Love* is the dazzling archetype. I think it is one of the most perfect novels ever written; one of its more masterly aspects is the way in which its author implies the enormous gap between a girl of twenty-one and a boy of sixteen. In *Twelfth Night*, when Viola, dressed as one of the Duke's pages, is sent to Olivia to plead her master's suit, the whole scene reeks of unrequited love, but also of being stricken at first sight; Viola for the Duke, about whom she is really speaking, Olivia for the eloquent boy, Viola.

Everyone has heard of Dante and Beatrice: perhaps it will come as a shock to some to hear that he first saw and adored his lady when he was nine.

Nancy Mitford has a wonderfully light touch. I should like to explode a nasty little highbrow theory here. The fact that this episode describes what a great many women would *like* to have happen to them, does not in any way depreciate its authenticity or its literary value. I am not talking about French dukes and the English upper class, but about an intensely romantic woman encountering for the first time a man who immediately and violently attracts her. The people who dismiss this kind of writing (and they are many and there is not much of it) as escapism, are, I think, merely envious. Vicarious pleasure is the next best thing to the direct kind: being agonized or bored at the kitchen sink or tortured by the KGB are not morally superior alternatives.

I want to mention the pieces from *A Game of Hide and Seek* by Elizabeth Taylor because I regard her as one of the best novelists of the century, and also the most underrated from the popular point of view. This novel is imbued with first love: Mrs Taylor has caught the languor, the pioneering with worldliness, the sharp and innocent curiosity of the very young experimenting in each other's company with such poetic accuracy and apparent ease that she can afford to be very funny about it. No mean feat; as most of us in the business know, apparent ease equates with extraordinarily hard work and/or virtuosity.

Finally, I have included a piece of my own work because it seemed apposite and I liked it.

The Finding of Love

Pale at first and cold,
Like wizard's lily-bloom
Conjured from the gloom,
Like torch of glow-worm seen
Through grasses shining green
By children half in fright,
Or Christmas candlelight
Flung on the outer snow,
Or tinsel stars that show
Their evening glory
With sheen of fairy story—

Now with his blaze
Love dries the cobweb maze
Dew-sagged upon the corn,
He brings the flowering thorn,
Mayfly and butterfly,
And pigeons in the sky,
Robin and thrush,
And the long bulrush,
The cherry under the leaf,
Earth in a silken dress,
With end to grief,
With joy in steadfastness.

ROBERT GRAVES

First Love

The following encounter—although not the first between them—encapsulates the feeling between the sixteen year old Vladimir and Princess Zinaida who is five years older than he. She is his first love: disastrously in love herself with a much older man (mercifully he does not know whom) and she regards Vladimir merely as a nice, attentive child.

One day I was sitting on the wall staring into space, and listening to the bells chiming. Suddenly something went through me, softer than the gentlest puff of wind, scarcely a shiver, like a scarcely perceptible breath, the sense of someone's presence. I looked down. Below—on the road—in a light grey dress, with a pink parasol resting on her shoulder, Zinaida was walking quickly. She saw me, stopped, and turning back the brim of her straw hat, she lifted her velvet eyes towards me.

'What are you doing so high up there?' she asked me with an odd smile. 'Now you always declare,' she went on, 'that you love me. Well, then, jump down into the road to me, if you truly love me.'

Hardly had Zinaida spoken these words when I was falling through the air, just as if someone had pushed me from behind. The wall was about fourteen feet high. I touched the ground with my feet, but the impact was so strong that I could not keep my balance. I fell flat and for an instant lost consciousness. When I came to, still without opening my eyes, I felt Zinaida near me.

'My darling boy,' she was saying, bending over me, and her voice was full of tender anxiety. 'How could you do it? How could you listen to me? When you know I love you . . . Oh, please stand up.'

Her bosom rose and fell beside me; her hands were touching my head and suddenly—oh, what became of me then?—her soft fresh lips began to cover my face with kisses. She touched my lips, but then Zinaida probably realized from the expression on my face that I had regained consciousness, although I still kept my eyes closed, and rising quickly, she said: 'Come, get up, you naughty boy, you idiot. Why are you lying in the dust?'

I got up.

'Give me my parasol,' said Zinaida. 'See where I have thrown

4

it. Don't look at me like that—it is too ridiculous. You aren't hurt, are you? Stung by the nettles, I expect . . . I tell you, don't look at me . . . why, he doesn't understand a word, he doesn't answer,' she said, as if to herself. 'Go home, Monsieur Woldemar, and tidy yourself up, and don't you dare follow me, or I shall be furious, and will never again . . .'

She did not finish her sentence, and moved quickly away. I sank down on the road. My legs would not carry me. My arms were smarting from the nettles, my back ached, my head swam, but at that moment I experienced a sense of bliss such as I never again felt in the whole of my life. It flowed like a delicious pain through all my limbs and finally resolved itself in rapturous leaps and cries. Yes, indeed, I was still a child.

I felt so gay and proud all that day. I retained so vividly the sensation of Zinaida's kisses on my face—I recollected her every word with such ecstasy of delight, I nursed my unexpected happiness so tenderly, that I even suffered moments of anxiety in which I would actually have preferred never to see again the author of these new sensations. It seemed to me that there was nothing more I could ask of fate, that one might now 'go, take a deep, sweet, final breath and die'. And yet, on the next day, when I made my way to the lodge, I felt great embarrassment which I tried vainly to conceal by putting on the kind of modest yet quietly self-assured expression of someone who wished to convey that he can keep a secret. Zinaida received me very simply, without the slightest emotion. She merely shook her finger at me and asked whether I wasn't black and blue all over. All my modest self-assurance and air of mystery instantly dissolved, and with them my embarrassment. I did not, of course, expect anything extraordinary, but Zinaida's calm was like a cold douche. I realized that I was a child in her eyes, and my heart sank. Zinaida walked up and down in the room, giving me a quick smile every time she glanced at me; but her thoughts were far away—that I saw clearly.

Shall I begin about yesterday myself, I thought, and ask her where she was hurrying, and find out once and for all? . . . But I couldn't; I let it pass, and humbly sat down in a corner.

IVAN TURGENEV

The Pursuit of Love

Linda, having left her second husband in the arms of a welfare worker in Spain, arrives exhausted and unhappy at the Gare du Nord in Paris, only to find her return ticket to England has expired, she possesses 6s 3d, is famished and knows nobody in Paris. A Frenchman in a black hat approaches her, laughing.

'*Bonjour, bonjour*', he said.

'*Voulez-vous vous en aller?*' said Linda, rather more doubtfully, here at least was a human being who showed signs of taking some interest in her. Then she thought of South America.

'*Il faut expliquer que je ne suis pas,*' she said, '*une esclave blanche. Je suis la fille d'un très important lord anglais.*'

The Frenchman gave a great bellow of laughter.

'One does not,' he said in the nearly perfect English of somebody who has spoken it from a child, 'have to be Sherlock Holmes to guess that.'

Linda was rather annoyed. An Englishwoman abroad may be proud of her nationality and her virtue without wishing them to jump so conclusively to the eye.

'French ladies,' he went on, 'covered with *les marques extérieurs de la richesse* never never sit crying on their suitcases at the Gare du Nord in the very early morning, while *esclaves blanches* always have protectors, and it is only too clear that you are unprotected just now.'

This sounded all right, and Linda was mollified.

'Now,' he said, 'I invite you to luncheon with me, but first you must have a bath and rest and a cold compress on your face.'

He picked up her luggage and walked to a taxi.

'Get in, please.'

Linda got in. She was far from certain that this was not the road to Buenos Aires, but something made her do as he said. Her powers of resistance were at an end, and she really saw no alternative.

'Hotel Montalembert,' he told the taxi man. 'Rue du Bac. *Je m'excuse, madame,* for not taking you to the Ritz, but I have a feeling for the Hotel Montalembert just now, that it will suit your mood this morning.'

Linda sat upright in her corner of the taxi, looking, she hoped, very prim. As she could not think of anything pertinent to say she remained silent. Her companion hummed a little tune, and seemed vastly amused. When they arrived at the hotel, he took a room for her, told the liftman to show her to it, told the *concierge* to send her up a *café complet*, kissed her hand, and said:

'*A tout à l'heure*—I will fetch you a little before one o'clock and we will go out to luncheon.'

Linda had her bath and breakfast and got into bed. When the telephone bell rang she was so sound asleep that it was a struggle to wake up.

'*Un monsieur qui demande madame.*'

'*Je descends tout de suite*,' said Linda, but it took her quite half an hour to get ready.

'Ah! You keep me waiting,' he said, kissing her hand, or at least making a gesture of raising her hand towards his lips and then dropping it rather suddenly. 'That is a very good sign.'

'Sign of what?' said Linda. He had a two-seater outside the hotel and she got into it. She was feeling more like herself again.

'Oh, of this and that,' he said, letting in the clutch, 'a good augury for our affair, that it will be happy and last long.'

Linda became intensely stiff, English and embarrassed, and said, self-consciously:

'We are not having an affair.'

'My name is Fabrice—may one ask yours?'

'Linda.'

'Linda. *Comme c'est joli*. With me, it usually lasts five years.'

He drove to a restaurant where they were shown, with some deference, to a table in a red plush corner. He ordered the luncheon and the wine in rapid French, the sort of French that Linda frankly could not follow, then, putting his hands on his knees, he turned to her and said:

'*Allons, racontez, madame.*'

'*Racontez* what?'

'Well, but of course, the story. Who was it that left you to cry on that suitcase?'

'He didn't. I left him. It was my second husband and I have left him for ever because he has fallen in love with another woman—a welfare worker, not that you'd know what that is, because I'm sure they don't exist in France. It just makes it worse, that's all.'

'What a very curious reason for leaving one's second husband. Surely with your experience of husbands you must have noticed that falling in love with other women is one of the things they do? However, it's an ill wind, and I don't complain. But why the suitcase? Why didn't you put yourself in the train and go back to Monsieur the important lord, your father?'

'That's what I was doing until they told me that my return ticket had expired. I only had 6s. 3d., and I don't know anybody in Paris, and I was awfully tired, so I cried.'

'The second husband—why not borrow some money from him? Or had you left a note on his pillow—women never can resist these little essays in literature, and they do make it rather embarrassing to go back, I know.'

'Well, anyhow he's in Perpignan, so I couldn't have.'

'Ah, you come from Perpignan. And what were you doing there, in the name of heaven?'

'In the name of heaven we were trying to stop you frogs from teasing the poor Epagnards,' said Linda with some spirit.

'E-spa-gnols! So we are teasing them, are we?'

'Not so badly now—terribly at the beginning.'

'What were we supposed to do with them? We never invited them to come, you know.'

'You drove them into camps in that cruel wind, and gave them no shelter for weeks. Hundreds died.'

'It is quite a job to provide shelter, at a moment's notice, for half a million people. We did what we could—we fed them— the fact is that most of them are still alive.'

'Still herded in camps.'

'My dear Linda, you could hardly expect us to turn them loose on the countryside with no money—what would be the result? Do use your common sense.'

'You should mobilize them to fight in the war against Fascism that's coming any day now.'

'Talk about what you know and you won't get so angry. We haven't enough equipment for our own soldiers in the war against Germany that's coming—not any day, but after the harvest, probably in August. Now go on telling me about your husbands. It's so very much more interesting.'

'Only two. My first was a Conservative, and my second is a Communist.'

'Just as I guessed, your first is rich, your second is poor. I could see you once had a rich husband, the dressing-case and the fur coat, though it is a hideous colour, and no doubt, as far as one could see, with it bundled over your arm, a hideous shape. Still, *vison* usually betokens a rich husband somewhere. Then this dreadful linen suit you are wearing has ready-made written all over it.'

'You are rude, it's a very pretty suit.'

'And last year's. Jackets are getting longer you will find. I'll get you some clothes—if you were well dressed you would be quite good-looking, though it's true your eyes are small. Blue, a good colour, but small.'

'In England,' said Linda, 'I am considered a beauty.'

'Well, you have points.'

So this silly conversation went on and on, but it was only froth on the surface. Linda was feeling, what she had never so far felt for any man, an overwhelming physical attraction. It made her quite giddy, it terrified her. She could see that Fabrice was perfectly certain of the outcome, so was she perfectly certain, and that was what frightened her. How could she, Linda, with the horror and contempt she had always felt for casual affairs, allow herself to be picked up by any stray foreigner, and, having seen him only for an hour, long and long and long to be in bed with him? He was not even good-looking, he was exactly like dozens of other dark men in Homburgs that can be seen in the streets of any French town. But there was something about the way he looked at her which seemed to be depriving her of all balance. She was profoundly shocked, and, at the same time, intensely excited.

NANCY MITFORD

Twelfth Night (Act I, Sc v)

Viola, dressed as a boy and in service to the Duke Orsino, has been sent by him to sue on his behalf for the love of Olivia. Every line of this scene is redolent of discovering love: of Viola's for the Duke; of Olivia's for Viola.

. . . .

VIOLA: I see you what you are, you are too proud;

9

But, if you were the devil, you are fair.
My lord and master loves you: O, such love
Could be but recompensed, though you were
   crown'd
The nonpareil of beauty!

OLIVIA: How does he love me?

VIOLA: With adorations, fertile tears,
With groans that thunder love, with sighs of fire.

OLIVIA: Your lord does know my mind; I cannot love him:
Yet I suppose him virtuous, know him noble,
Of great estate, of fresh and stainless youth;
In voices well divulged, free, learn'd and valiant;
And in dimension and the shape of nature
A gracious person: but yet I cannot love him;
He might have took his answer long ago.

VIOLA: If I did love you in my master's flame,
With such a suffering, such a deadly life,
In your denial I would find no sense;
I would not understand it.

OLIVIA: Why, what would you?

VIOLA: Make me a willow cabin at your gate,
And call upon my soul within the house;
Write loyal canons of contemned love
And sing them loud even in the dead of night;
Halloo your name to the reverberate hills,
And make the babbling gossip of the air
Cry out 'Olivia!' O, you should not rest
Between the elements of air and earth,
But you should pity me!

OLIVIA: You might do much.
What is your parentage?

VIOLA: Above my fortunes, yet my state is well:
I am a gentleman.

OLIVIA: Get you to your lord;
I cannot love him: let him send no more;
Unless, perchance, you come to me again,
To tell me how he takes it. Fare you well:
I thank you for your pains: spend this for me.

VIOLA: I am no fee'd post, lady; keep your purse:
My master, not myself, lacks recompense.
Love make his heart of flint that you shall love;
And let your fervour, like my master's, be
Placed in contempt! Farewell, fair cruelty.   [*Exit*]
OLIVIA: 'What is your parentage?'
'Above my fortunes, yet my state is well:
I am a gentleman.' I'll be sworn thou art;
Thy tongue, thy face, thy limbs, actions, and
    spirit,
Do give thee five-fold blazon: not too fast: soft,
    soft!
Unless the master were the man. How now!
Even so quickly may one catch the plague?

WILLIAM SHAKESPEARE

Bettina: A Portrait

*Bettina Brentano is best known for her extraordinary relation-
ship with Goethe about whom she published a book. The
following incident occurred during the warfare between the
Austrians and Napoleon. This is probably the occasion described by Bettina in a letter to Goethe apropos of her emotions
on being kissed.*

Our summer life was suddenly disturbed by scenes of warfare. There was no time for flight; when we woke up in the
morning, the cry was 'Down to the cellar'; the town was under
fire; the French had entered and the Redmantles [Hungarian
Cavalry officered by Austrians] and the Deathsheads [Austrian
Hussars] were attacking on all sides to drive them out. People
ran to and fro in the streets telling each other about the Redmantles, how they gave no quarter, hacked everyone down, how
they had fearful moustaches, rolling eyes, and their mantles
were red to hide the blood stains. Soon shutters were closed and
the streets emptied; the first cannon ball sent everyone down to

the cellar; there we sat while the time passed slowly; after a time a bomb burst in our court; that was a diversion but now there was the danger of fire; my grandmother thought of her valuable pictures and books, and wanted to get them down into the cellar; the manservant maintained that it was impossible to get St. John, a picture which had the remarkable quality of being able to prove that it was a Raphael, down from the sitting room as it was too heavy; before they had finished arguing I had slipped out of the room, gone up the stairs, got the heavy picture by its cord over my back, and clattered down again to the cellar. I assured them that I had looked out of the drawing room window and everything was quiet in the street, I was given the key of the library to rescue the books of engravings; I was delighted to be allowed into the library, it contained a collection of beautiful shells and dried plants and on the walls were old weapons, ostriches' eggs, and a loadstone on which knitting needles would remain attached; there were dressing tables with wonderful old crockery and ornaments, aigrettes and stars of coloured stones and diamonds. I took downstairs the things which grandmother wanted and was looking forward to a quiet night examining all these treasures when the shooting began again; a single horseman in full gallop broke the alarming silence of the street; several times I heard a rider pass. 'Perhaps it is a Redmantle'; I thought, and running to the ground floor window I opened the shutters; there he was galloping down the street with his mantle flying out behind, drawn sabre and long flowing moustaches, thick black pigtails appearing from his red fur shako; dead silence followed; then I saw a young man in shirt sleeves, bareheaded, deathly pale, bespattered with blood, running despairingly to and fro and knocking on house doors and shutters, but nobody opened to him; I signalled to him; at first he could not see me; then he ran up to me in entreaty; a horse's hoofs rang out; he crouched in the darkness of the courtyard door; a horseman looking for fugitives dashed up, stopped nearby and looked into the distance, then turned and went. Every glance and movement of the horseman and his horse had burnt into my brain; the frightened youth swung up on my arm through the window but again a soldier rode past, and seeing me approached and asked for water; I fetched it from the kitchen and when he had ridden off I looked at my prisoner; if the soldier had stood up in his stirrups he would have seen him. I closed the shutters and looked down at him; trembling he kissed my hands; 'Oh, mon dieu, mon dieu, sauvez moi, cachez moi, mon père et ma mère prieront pour vous': I took his hands and led him to the woodshed. There I examined his wounds; I could not wash off the blood, as I did not dare to fetch water because our neighbour Andree had climbed up to his lookout to see how the war was going and would notice me; the only thing I could do was to lick the wounds clean: I was carefully drawing aside the matted hair, when a hen flew down with a squawk from the woodpile, we had frightened it from the place where it laid its eggs. I climbed up, got the egg, and put the white over the wound; it may possibly have healed it, I hope so; I went back to the cellar; one sister was asleep the other was praying; grandmother was making her will at a little table, and the aunt was making tea. I fetched the key of the larder, and brought out wine and cold food, and took some to my poor prisoner. So the day passed and with it the danger. We left the cellar and my secret became more difficult to keep. I had to watch every step of the household, I fetched wood and water for the cook on the excuse that it might be dangerous for her. At last night came; a neighbour brought news that there was nothing more to fear for the moment, so we could get the rest we needed. I had to find civilian clothes for my prisoner; how fortunate that I had left the library unlocked, I remembered that there was a sportsman's coat and cap of some past period hanging there; I used to keep all my allowance, which I had no occasion to use, in the cushions of a leathern chair; I dug in the chair and found an adequate supply of ready money which I handed to my protege for his travelling expenses; I led him through the moonlit, scented garden; we went slowly, hand in hand, beyond the row of willows to the rose hedge where the nightingale used to build. He took me in his arms and lifted me high, kissed me, and climbed over the rose hedge into the garden that leads down to the Main; he would be able to cross as there were boats on the bank. There are unexpected events which one forgets as if they had never been, only when they rise out of the well of memory, does one realize their real meaning. It is as if things happen in order to teach one their importance. Events, on the other hand, to which one looks forward with enthusiasm pass away like running water.

When you asked me who gave me the first kiss which I remembered, my memory rushed to and fro like a weaver's shuttle until I saw clearly before me the face of the man I had saved, and in this recall of emotion I was conscious for the first time of the deep effect which the kiss had made.

ARTHUR HELPS:
ELIZABETH JANE HOWARD

Dante and Beatrice

It was at the end of his ninth year that Dante first saw Beatrice, who was almost a year younger, wearing a dress of delicate crimson. His pounding heart at once formed the words: 'Behold a god stronger than I who comes to rule over me.' And indeed from that moment he was Love's willing servant, forever seeking to catch a glimpse of this angel of tender years and seeing her inspiring image continually before him. It was nine years later that he met her in the street in the company of two older women. This time she was dressed in pure white and turned to give him a greet'ng, which filled him with such joy that he fled to the privacy of his room; and there, with his thoughts fixed on her, he fell asleep.

In a dream he saw a cloud the colour of fire, and in that cloud a lordly figure, awe-inspiring yet seeming imbued with great joy. It spoke to him these words: 'I am your master.' In its arms lay the sleeping Beatrice, wrapped lightly in a crimson cloth; and in one hand it held a fiery object. 'See here your heart,' it said. Then, waking the sleeping girl, it made her, despite her misgivings, eat the burning object. Soon after, its joy turned to bitter grief; and taking the girl once more into its arms, it seemed to ascend into the heavens. At this Dante felt such anguish that he woke. For the benefit of his fellow-poets he recounted his vision in sonnet form and asked for an interpretation. One came from Guido Cavalcanti; and from that time the two men's friendship was formed.

After his vision Dante grew weak from love, and his friends remarked on his changed appearance. However, though he admitted the nature of his malady, he would not disclose his lady's name. In church one day he found himself placed so that he could look at his beloved. Between them sat another lady, and those who followed his gaze thought it was directed at her, not Beatrice. Dante encouraged this belief for several years, even composing some verses for this pretended love and, when she left Florence, a lament. Whom could he now use as a cover for his real passion? He seemed to see the God of Love appear to him again, bringing back the heart he had taken to the other and about to carry it for lodging with a further lady, who was now to become his screen.

His new pretence was too successful. Beatrice's greeting, which was for him the source of purest joy, was on one occasion refused. It was for sorrow that Dante now withdrew to his room, where he could weep alone like a beaten child. Sleep came, and with it another dream in which the Lord of Love appeared, dressed all in white. Dante must dissemble no longer. Word had reached Beatrice that he had given some cause for annoyance to the lady who was now his screen; and fearing she might receive the same, Beatrice had withheld her greeting. So now Dante must compose for her a song in which the truth of his love would be told and be recognised by her. This song he soon wrote, and then a sonnet speaking of his vacillating thoughts about love.

It happened that Dante was taken by a friend to visit one newly-wed who was entertaining a number of ladies. Having joined the company, he felt in the left side of his breast a sudden throbbing that quickly spread to his whole body. He leant against a wall to steady himself and, raising his eyes, he saw Beatrice among the guests. The sight routed all his senses, so that his friend was forced to lead him away, while some of the ladies mocked his behaviour in the hearing of Beatrice. Returning to his room of tears, he addressed a new sonnet to her, explaining the cause of his senses' disarray, then two further poems where he again told of his confusion as Love waged its battle within him. Now it became clear to some people who Dante's beloved was; and one day a group of ladies taxed him with loving her whose presence he could not endure. His reply was that formerly his highest desire was to be greeted by her; but now she has denied him this blessing, his whole joy lies in singing his lady's praises. So to this he turns, claiming that Heaven's only lack is the absence of so perfect a creature. A sonnet follows on the theme 'Love and the noble heart are one selfsame thing', and another speaks of the ennobling quality of his own lady, such a miracle of grace is she.

A Game of Hide and Seek

Vesey has been—very casually—invited to go for a walk with Harriet. They are both about eighteen. Their mothers are old friends.

For the first ten minutes they were explaining to one another why they had chosen to go for this walk together. Boredom had driven them to it, they decided; a fear, on Vesey's part, lest he should be asked by Hugo to mow and mark the tennis-lawn; a wish, on Harriet's part, to collect wild-flowers for the children to draw. If the walk turned out badly, it could be the fault of neither, for neither had desired it nor attached importance to it. In a few years' time, they would be dissembling the other way; professing pleasure they did not feel, undreamed of eagerness. They had not yet learned to gush. Their protestations were of an oafish kind.

When they had established their lack of interest in being together, they became silent. Harriet gathered a large bunch of quaking-grass from under a hedge. Vesey kicked a stone down the middle of the road.

'If only,' Harriet thought, 'there were no *women* at universities! If only they still were not allowed!' (Her mother once had taken tea at Girton with Miss Emily Davies. It had seemed to her well worth going to prison to have been so rewarded.)

But Harriet saw Vesey lying in a punt, his fingers trailing in the water as he watched through lids half-closed against the sun a young woman who was reading Ernest Dowson to him. Her imagination excused Vesey from any exertion, as probability did also. The boat drifted as if by magic past Bablock-Hythe and under Godstow Bridge towards the Aegean Isles. And all this time, Harriet herself sat at the schoolroom-table typing Caroline's letters; for pocket money.

Vesey, whose next steps would take him over the threshold of a new and promising world, wished to go without any backward glances or entanglements. He was not one to keep up friendships, never threw out fastening tendrils such as letters or presents or remembrances; was quite unencumbered by all the things which Harriet valued and kept: drawers full of photographs, brochures, programmes, postcards, diaries. He never remembered birthdays or any other anniversary.

Although he was ambitious at this time to become a great writer, he saw himself rather as a literary figure than as a man at work. At school, he had often turned to the index of a History of Literature and in his mind inserted his own name—Vesey Patrick Macmillan—between Machiavelli and Sir Thomas Malory.

'Everything seems so certain for you,' Harriet said, as they toiled up the side of a hill towards a wood. 'So uncertain for me.'

'In what way?'

He stopped with a hand against his lower ribs, out of condition as his Uncle Hugo never had been in his life.

'That you are going to Oxford, and can pass exams.'

'Exams are nothing,' he said. ("They do not seem to be," Harriet thought, "to those who pass them.")

Both wanted to sit down in the shade at the edge of the woods: neither would suggest it.

'And then you'll be a schoolmaster and have a great deal of money,' Harriet said without irony, her mind on her own pittance.

'A schoolmaster?'

Vesey stopped dead, holding back a long springing branch so that she could go by. 'Why do you say that?'

'It is what I heard Caroline say.'

He had not held the branch quite long enough and Harriet now disentangled it from her hair.

'She would! These old-time suffragettes!' Vesey said tactlessly. 'They are only happy if they can see men in a subservient position.'

Harriet could not see that it was in the least a subservient position. She could scarcely imagine more authority or scope.

'Then what will you do?' she asked.

'I have never told anybody, but I mean to be a writer.'

Harriet flushed; both at the confidence and at the nature of it. She bent down hastily and began to tug at some bracken to add to her bunch.

'To write novels?' she asked.

He preferred the more oblong shapes of books on literary criticism, belles lettres. To become a man of letters, he would make special to himself one smallish aspect of literature, read all the books about it, add another of his own. Anything later encroaching on his territory, he would himself review.

'The novel is practically finished as an art form,' he replied.

'I suppose it is,' said Harriet.

'Virginia Woolf has brought it to the edge of ruin.'

'Yes,' said Harriet.

'But it was inevitable,' he added, laying no blame.

'I suppose it was,' Harriet said, in a slow, considering way. The novel—headstrong parvenu—seemed headed for destruction. No one could stay its downward course and, obviously, it did not deserve that Vesey should try. Virginia Woolf with one graceful touch after another (the latest was *Mrs Dalloway*) was sending it trundling downhill. She had been doing this unbeknown to Harriet who had never even heard of her.

She had wished to include her own future in their discussion and he had not given it a glance. She sighed theatrically, but he failed to ask her why. Plunging through dead leaves, they were obliged to walk in single file, twigs snapped under their feet, briars tripped them. Cool and vast, the wood seemed a whole world; the light was aqueous; when a cuckoo gave its broken, explosive cry it echoed like a shout in a closed swimming-bath—for some reason, chilling and hysterical as those sounds are.

Vesey now had a blister on his heel. He sat down on the fine, transparent grass that grows beneath trees and took off his sandal. His foot was white and veined and rather dirty. He rested it in the cool grass and leaned back against the trunk of a tree. Harriet stood awkwardly before him, feeling too tall.

'Have you a handkerchief?' she asked.

'No.' He smiled. He looked rather fagged, as if this evening stroll had been too much for him.

If only her own handkerchief were of the finest cambric, smelling of flowers! She took out a crumpled cotton one left over from schooldays, with 'Harriet Claridge' printed clumsily along the hem.

'Why "Harriet", I wonder,' Vesey asked, reading it. 'Though it is quite a pretty name.'

'It was after Harriet Martineau.'

'Ah, yes, of course.' He smiled again.

'I could tie it for you.'

'I cannot bear anyone to touch my feet.'

She rearranged her bunch of flowers and held them out at arm's length to consider them.

'None the less, sit down beside me,' he presently said.

Surprised, she hesitated, then sat down rather round the tree from him so that they must talk slightly over their shoulders. Her hands, at her side, pressed into dry twigs, the empty cases of last year's beech-nuts.

'I hope you will be very happy, very famous,' she said. To say this more easily she laid an edge of mockery to her voice.

Her brown, ink-smudged hand pressed down into the dead leaves drew his attention. Looking sideways, he examined it carefully.

'Thank you,' he said, and his voice, too, sank into mockery. She could not allow to him the same motive as her own and, imagining he had wished to rebuke her, pointed out that it was time to go home. 'Or you will be late for supper,' she said, as if he were intolerably preoccupied with meals.

Nervously, tenderly, he put his own hand over hers.

'*You* will be late too,' he said, as if nothing had happened.

'My mother . . . ' she began; but she could not continue. She seemed to have stepped over into another world; confused, as though the demarcation had been between life and death, she imagined herself swimming, floating, in a strange element where hearing and sight no longer existed.

'Your mother what . . .?' he asked. He slid his hand up her arm and into her sleeve.

She could not remember what she had been about to say. Watching a velvety grey spider crossing her ankle, she was surprised that she did not experience her usual fear and disgust.

Vesey had turned to face her and the tree. She had never seen his face so close to her own, nor dared to look at him as she looked now. He drew her away from the tree into his arms and rested his head against her, and still she could not move but was locked up in amazement and disbelief. Only when he loosened her, as he soon did, sensing her constraint, did she begin to relax, to tremble. She raised her hands stiffly. Pieces of twig, small stones, were pressed into the creased and reddened palms. She brushed them on her skirt and stared about her. Then a great silence, of despair, ennui, disappointment with herself, widened in her, like a yawn. The trees seemed to march away from her into the darkness; the wood was a chilly vault, the birds had stopped calling. Vesey sat beside her still, prising bits of white flint out of the mossy earth with a stick which kept snapping. Absorbed, he did this. Fatally, she covered her face with her hands.

'What is wrong?' he asked gently.

He drew her hands away and kissed her cheek. In spite of his seeming assurance, he was not really sure.

'Harriet?'

'Yes, Vesey?'

'Have I done wrong?'

'No.'

The yawn, the disappointment was contagious. Touching her again, his excitement undiminished, he was at the same time reminded of the dullness of consequences. The tears which she had not let fall cautioned him. He began to wonder if violent embraces are not often induced by not knowing what to do next, of losing one's nerve as much as losing one's control. He put his sandal on again, easing it with elaborate care over the bandage, frowning, as he buckled it.

'It is only . . .' she began unpromisingly (that daunting opening to long complaints, long confessions) 'only that sometimes I worry about the future. And hearing you to-night . . . so sure . . . there is nothing for *me* to do, as there is for you. I wonder what will happen to me . . .'

Relief made him robust.

'Someone will marry you,' he cruelly said. He stood up and brushed leaves away, then he put out his hand to help her to her feet.

. . . .

In a café one afternoon, he saw a little girl who reminded him of Harriet as a child. Her long hair straggled over her shoulders, her thin arms were covered by a tight jersey. She sat at a table with her father and two younger children. When the tea was brought, her father nodded at her with a casual and flattering gesture. Colour rode up in her cheeks. She stood up and lifted the tea-pot with two hands. Vesey could see that the father, so apparently relaxed, was ready to spring to her rescue. The wobbly stream of tea descended into his cup. He took it from her with careless thanks. She smiled. She shone with relief. 'This is my first time,' she said, 'of pouring out.' Vesey looked away. He felt a personal guilt towards the grave, successful and beloved little girl, besides a tardy guilt towards Harriet. 'Love is not difficult,' he thought. In the child's father it had seemed the simplest thing, as was the expression of it. He began to hope that the mother was merely resting for the afternoon, and not dead. But having seen so much happiness, he desired more. He imagined the mother at home in child-birth. 'I will take the children out to tea,' the husband had said. When they returned, he would run upstairs. He would be excited, not anxious, over his fourth child. He would call to his daughter to come and see. Going sedately upstairs, with her self-conscious little smile, she would imagine a wonderful future, not just pouring out tea, but of pushing prams, of straightening the baby every yard or so and plumping up his pillow, so that he would be a credit to her. 'But perhaps after all the mother is dead,' he thought, as he paid his bill. 'Perhaps it is their first holiday without her. He is trying hard: and succeeding much better than those who think they have no need to try.'

ELIZABETH TAYLOR

Héloïse and Abélard

Héloïse, who as a young girl had unusual zeal for scholarship, was the reason for Abélard getting lodgings in her uncle's house. He agreed to teach her, but, initially, this was simply with a view to her seduction. Her immediate whole-hearted love for him, however, transformed the situation, and though she was supposed to be his pupil, the curriculum was wider than was supposed. This is Abélard in a later confession to a friend.

With study as our pretext, we made ourselves wholly free for love, and our lessons provided the furtive privacy love desired; and so, though our books lay open, more words of love prevailed than of instruction, more kisses than precepts. Hands moved more frequently to breasts than to the books. Love turned our gaze more often into each other's eyes than reading kept it on the text. And sometimes, the better to avoid suspicion, I gave her blows, but of love not anger, of affection not wrath, and sweeter they were than any balm. What more can I say? In our passion we omitted none of the steps lovers take, and if there was anything less usual our love might devise, that too we accomplished. And the less versed we had been in those delights, the more ardently we pursued them, and the less sated we became.

My Young Years

'Would you play something for me?' she whispered in a low, soft voice. 'Gladly', I answered, and we went to the piano. Her husband stopped talking and settled himself comfortably on the little sofa, and she pushed one of the armchairs nearer to the piano.

'What will you play?' she asked, putting a vase with dark red roses on the side of the piano stand.

'Something of Chopin,' and I began to play the long D flat Nocturne as though in a trance, inspired by her beauty. The Count closed his eyes; when his chin dropped, a barely audible soft snore announced that he was asleep. When I reached the coda with its pianissimo descending sighs, the Countess, suddenly, leaned forward close to me and, covered by the open stand and the flowers, kissed my mouth with a wild passion. I struck a wrong note, too loudly—the Count woke up, and the charm was broken. We finished our champagne, I kissed her hand several times, with ardor; the Count accompanied me to the door, and I left the house. I never saw either of them again.

ARTHUR RUBINSTEIN

Something in Disguise

Elizabeth, who is twenty and works as an evening cook, has just cleared up. The middle-aged John Cole—employing her for the first time—is taking his drunken ex-wife home. Apart from getting extremely drunk, Mrs Cole appeared desperately unhappy and Elizabeth has become anxious and frightened of Mr Cole.

There was absolutely no reason, she went on, wildly, why on earth stupid people shouldn't be wicked: it was far more likely, when you came to consider it. It was supposed to be far easier to be wicked than to be good, and Oliver had said that one of the hallmarks of stupid people was that they always did what they thought was the easiest thing: the fact that it often turned out not to be that was neither here nor there . . .

The front door slammed: why hadn't she *left*? She seized her bag and basket, turned out the kitchen lights, and almost ran up the basement stairs, straight into John Cole at the top.

She ran into him with such force that if he had not caught hold of her shoulder, she would have lost her balance and fallen back down the stairs.

'Steady.'

'I'm going home now.'

'Hang on a minute.'

'I've got to go—honestly.'

But a strand of her hair seemed to have got caught in one of his waistcoat buttons: she jerked, and tore the tangled hairs out by their roots with half a dozen little dwarf mandrake screams of agony. Tears filled her eyes.

'Steady,' he said again, but more seriously.

He took her upper arm and walked her through the nearest door.

'Don't *frog*march me!'

He laughed. 'I couldn't be doing that: you have to be four to one for that. I'm leading you to the nearest comfortable chair which is what one does to girls in your condition.' He pushed her gently into it, and took the basket from her.

'There you are. I say, that's Little Red Riding Hood equipment. Had you suddenly decided that I was a good old-fashioned wolf— look here, what *is* it?'

For the moment she sat down, tears began spurting from her eyes. For a few seconds she glared unseeingly at him, too offended with herself even to search for a handkerchief. He went to the other side of the room and came back with a tumbler so heavy that her hand shook with surprise at its weight.

'The male equivalent of a nice cup of tea,' he said.

'I don't like whisky.'

'As a matter of fact, it's brandy. Brandy and soda. I should have said the male nouveau riche equivalent of a nice cup of tea.'

She drank some, and then said, 'It's simply that things seem awful to me sometimes—nothing, really. Nothing to do with you,' she added, meaning to sound worldly, rather than rude. She gave him the glass to hold while she found her handkerchief, and then blew her nose in what she hoped was a practical and finishing-off manner.

'Have some more brandy. I'm going to have some too.' He handed her back her glass and went away again. It was a very large, dimly lit room, with two fireplaces and windows to the floor each end of it: it smelt of flowers and she was glad that it was dimly lit.

When he came back with his glass, he sat on the arm of a huge sofa near her chair and said, 'We've both had rather an awful evening. It's not surprising that you feel awful.'

'What about Mrs Cole?'

'Don't worry about her. *She's* all right.'

'She's *not* all right! She clearly wasn't at all all right!'

'She was stoned, of course. There's nothing unusual about that.'

Elizabeth was clutching her tumbler so hard that if it hadn't been made of plate-glass windows it would certainly have broken. She took a gulp of brandy for courage and said, 'She was extremely upset about someone called Jennifer.' She was watching him narrowly for a reaction.

'There's nothing unusual about that. She's been upset about Jennifer for years.

'Our daughter,' he added a moment later: and now it seemed to be the other way round—to be he who was watching her. Staring down at it, she was turning the glass round and round in her hands, and even with her fringe it was possible to see from the rest of her face that she was frowning. At last she said, 'Do you mean that she doesn't *know* where her *own* daughter lives?'

'That's right.'

'Who stops her knowing? You?'

'Yep.'

'That's monstrous!'

'Of course, sometimes my security slips up, but not if I can help it.'

'No wonder she is so dreadfully unhappy.'

'Yes, it's not a situation that makes for happiness—'

She got to her feet and looked wildly for somewhere to put her glass.

'I'm going home now.'

'You said that before.' But he rose to his feet and stood towering before her as he took her glass.

She looked defiantly up at him. 'Now I really *am*.'

He stood quite still watching her face. Then, with neat and gentle movements, he took off his glasses, folded them and put them in a pocket: without the glasses, he looked more simple, more serious, and inquiring. He put his arms round her, drew her towards him and put his mouth upon hers. They stayed like that for a long time, motionless and utterly silent.

Then they were both sitting on the sofa: he was holding one of her hands in both of his and speaking quite calmly—as though nothing had happened.

'You see, it's not only Daphne we have to consider: there's Jennifer, too. It got a bit much for her having her mother turn up without warning, dead drunk, falling all over the place at Speech Days and sometimes just any old day—anywhere. You know how conservative children are: well poor old Jennifer kept turning out to have a mother not like anybody else's mother. I had to put a stop to it. Daphne suffers from gusts of sentimental passion for Jennifer and there is nothing children hate more than that. Do you begin to see, at all?'

She nodded: she felt like two people: one inside, and one sitting on a sofa, talking. She said, 'But she can't always have been like this? She must somehow have *got* like it?'

'I don't know when that was. She'd been on the drink long before I met her. When I married her she came off it, because, poor girl, she thought I was going to love her in the way she wanted. But the trouble with alcoholics is that they can't love anyone back, you see: they're too taken up with themselves, and whether people are reassuring and loving them enough, and nobody ever can, so then they feel let down and switch the situation so that most of the letting down will be done by them. That's roughly it, I think. But it's an impossible situation for children: if you have them, you have to try and protect them from bad luck on that scale. I divorced her.'

He had put on his spectacles again, and was observing her, she found, when she looked up.

'Years ago.'

'How old is Jennifer?'

He reflected. 'Twenty in September.'

'I'm twenty.'

An expression she had not seen before crossed his face: then he said, 'That's why I explained this to you. I'm forty-five.'

There was a silence while they looked at each other. Then he took off his glasses again with one hand and put them on a table behind the sofa. 'I want to kiss you,' he said, and there ensued another unknown quantity of time and by the end of it she was lying on the sofa in the crook of one of his arms.

'Now is the moment for me to examine your face,' he said, 'I'm sorry to seem so fidgety, but that means putting on my spectacles.'

'Who cuts your hair?' he asked when they were on.

'My brother.'

'Good Lord!'

'He's not actually a hairdresser.'

'I can see that.' He pushed the hair out of her eyes. 'Anyway, with a forehead like that, it's a crime to have a fringe or bang or whatever it's called. Is it my imagination, or is your hair not perfectly dry?'

'It mightn't be. I'd just washed it when you rang up.'

'*Really*—may I call you Elizabeth? Well, *really*, Elizabeth!'

'It's all very well for *you*—'

'I was waiting for that.'

'How do you mean?'

'Some disparaging allusion to my baldness. Would it help if I told you that what hair I *have* got is incredibly greasy? A little of it goes a hell of a long way; you should be thankful it is so much on the decline.'

'I only meant that you *knew* when you are going to work, so you needn't get caught out washing your hair.' She sat up. 'Could I have my brandy?'

'In a minute; you're quite perky enough without it. Let me see your eyes.' He peered very close into her face and she could see two little Elizabeths—like Polyfotos—one in each lens.

'What marvellous, translucent whites you have—like a very young child. Or—let me see—thinly-sliced whites of hard-boiled egg—in case you think the young child stuff is a bit Dornford Yates.'

'Who's he?'

'When we have more time, I'll show you. True to form, I have nearly all of him in first editions upstairs. I'm afraid I've got to take off my glasses again.'

'I'll take them off.'

She leaned towards him as she did this and he kept perfectly still. He was staring at her mouth.

At last he took her head between his hands and began kissing her and this time it was different: it was not enough, and she could not bear it to stop. She clung to him and kissed him—the first time *she* had ever actually kissed in her life; afterwards, she flung her arms round his neck and rubbed her face against his to make the touching go on . . .

'I'm going to take you upstairs,' he said. He took her by the shoulders and pushed her a little away. 'Elizabeth: you've never done this before, have you?'

She shook her head. 'It's a kind of love—isn't it?'

'At first sight,' he said.

ELIZABETH JANE HOWARD

Part II

COURTSHIP, DECLARATIONS, STATEMENTS ABOUT LOVE

There are two stages of love when people become most communicative: when it has just begun, and when it is all over, or looks like being finished for one reason or another. There is so much material to choose from for these parts, that selection has been difficult, and in this category I have included general statements about love as well as particular declarations of it. Thus we have a piece from the Talmud, Carson McCullers' wonderful ruminations from *The Ballad of the Sad Café*, Bertrand Russell on the reasons for love and Robert Burton upon how it improves the lover, and the 'Code of Laws from the Courts of Love' that are as rich and varied as a good receipt for Christmas cake, but so much of the advice is ageless that one feels that even after nine hundred years most people would find parts of it handy.

There are six proposals of marriage, ranging through Jane Austen, Trollope, Wilde, Daisy Ashford and Queen Victoria. There is also the entrancing engagement between Kitty and Levin from *Anna Karenina* that has something uniquely warm and sunlit and golden about it, and at the same time is flooded with the joy that anybody who has ever been successfully in love can recognise. There are letters, passionate, plaintive, eloquent, funny, tender, pathetic; the interest here is that they were written for a particular person—a beloved audience of one. This is true, of course, of some poems, although it is more readily assumed in their case that they will eventually be published. Hardly anybody, however, with the possible exception of the Bloomsbury set (when, I suspect, a good deal of indoor posing went on) writes a serious love letter intending it for general perusal. There are poems here

28

that breathe of private life: 'Presents' by that virtuoso, Anon, might have been tucked inside a scented orange or tied to the leg of a robin redbreast; one can imagine something of what it must have felt like feeing a small boy for bringing Donne's 'Prohibition' or Shakespeare's caressingly peevish sonnet 'Being your slave what should I do but tend upon the hours and times of your desire?' There *are* poems here that do not have this private taste to them: Blake's 'Love's Secret', Betjeman's 'Olympic Girl', 'Feste's Song'; there are others that are enigmatic: Queen Elizabeth's 'Youth and Cupid', the Irish Song 'I know where I'm going' and 'Billy Boy'—in each case clearly for or about someone, but we shall never know who. There are songs, but there are also dances about love, as with C. Day Lewis' ravishingly rhythmic poems 'Jig' and 'Hornpipe'.

This part is full of optimism; a rising tide—declarations are hopeful things; it takes panache to wear one's heart in the right place—to learn that importunings require bravado as well as humility and grace. Even the statements about love hold the implicit promise that, if one obeys them, love will provide the kind of calm constancy of a Mediterranean summer.

Contents

Love's Secret

Never seek to tell thy love,
    Love that never told can be;
For the gentle wind doth move
    Silently, invisibly.

I told my love, I told my love,
    I told her all my heart,
Trembling, cold, in ghastly fears.
    Ah! She did depart!

Soon after she was gone from me,
    A traveller came by,
Silently, invisibly:
    He took her with a sigh.

WILLIAM BLAKE

Sir Richard Steele to Mary Scurlock (1707)

Madam,
   It is the hardest thing in the world to be in love and yet attend
to business. As for me, all who speak to me find me out, and I must
lock myself up or other people will do it for me.
   A gentleman asked me this morning, 'What news from Lisbon?'
and I answered, 'She is exquisitely handsome.' Another desired to
know when I had been last at Hampton Court. I replied, 'It will
be on Tuesday come se'nnight. Prythee, allow me at least to kiss
your hand before that day, that my mind may be in some composure. O love!—

        'A thousand torments dwell about me!
        Yet who would live to live without thee?'

   Methinks I could write a volume to you; but all the language on
earth would fail in saying how much and with what disinterested
passion I am ever yours,
                                        Rich. Steele

Love an Escape from Loneliness
(from Marriage and Morals)

Love is something far more than desire for sexual intercourse; it is the principal means of escape from the loneliness which afflicts most men and women throughout the greater part of their lives. There is a deep-seated fear, in most people, of the cold world and the possible cruelty of the herd; there is a longing for affection, which is often concealed by roughness, boorishness or a bullying manner in men, and by nagging and scolding in women. Passionate mutual love while it lasts puts an end to this feeling; it breaks down the hard walls of the ego, producing a new being composed of two in one. Nature did not construct human beings to stand alone, since they cannot fulfil her biological purpose except with the help of another; and civilized people cannot fully satisfy their sexual instinct without love. The instinct is not completely satisfied unless a man's whole being, mental quite as much as physical, enters into the relation. Those who have never known the deep intimacy and the intense companionship of happy mutual love have missed the best thing that life has to give; unconsciously, if not consciously, they feel this, and the resulting disappointment inclines them towards envy, oppression and cruelty. To give due place to passionate love should be therefore a matter which concerns the sociologist, since, if they miss this experience, men and women cannot attain their full stature, and cannot feel towards the rest of the world that kind of generous warmth without which their social activities are pretty sure to be harmful.

BERTRAND RUSSELL

Being Your Slave (Sonnet LVII)

Being your slave what should I do but tend,
Upon the hours and times of your desire?
I have no precious time at all to spend;
Nor services to do, till you require.
Nor dare I chide the world-without-end hour,
Whilst I (my sovereign) watch the clock for you,

Nor think the bitterness of absence sour,
When you have bid your servant once adieu.
Nor dare I question with my jealous thought,
Where you may be, or your affairs suppose.
But like a sad slave stay and think of nought
Save, where you are, how happy you make those,
    So true a fool is love that in your Will,
    (Though you do any thing) he thinks no ill.

WILLIAM SHAKESPEARE

The Code of Laws Common to all the Courts of Love in the English, the French, and the Provençal Dominions of the Twelfth Century

Marriage is not a justifiable plea for the refusal of love.
He who cannot keep a secret knows not how to love.
No one can devote himself to two loves.
Love is always either waxing or waning.
There is no true delight to the lover in what the loved one yields unwillingly.
A boy seldom loves until he has attained puberty.
If death should take one of two lovers, then love must be forsworn for two years by the lover that lives on.
No lover should be deprived of his privileges except for an excellent reason.
Love cannot be unless the persuasion of love itself compel it.
Where avarice keeps house love is in exile.
It is unbefitting to love a woman whom one would scorn to marry.
A true love longs for the embraces of the loved one only.
A love made commonplace seldom endures.
Too easy a success in love deprives it of its charm: hindrances add to its value.
A lover pales at sight of his beloved.
He trembles at an unforeseen meeting with her.
A new love banishes the old.

Worth alone makes one worthy of love.

As soon as love begins to languish, it quickly fades and seldom revives again.

A true lover is the constant prey of anxiety.

The passion of love frets into flame at the onset of jealousy.

Suspicion adds fuel to its fire.

Reverie and meditation on his love robs the lover both of appetite and sleep.

A lover's every action leads to thoughts of the loved one.

A true lover can find no pleasure except in that which he knows delights his beloved.

Love can deny love nothing.

No true lover is ever surfeited by the favours of his beloved.

The faintest distrust breeds evil suspicion.

An habitual and excessive pursuit of pleasure hinders the birth of love.

A true lover is haunted by the image of the loved one without any intermission, on and on.

There is nothing to prevent a woman from being loved by two men or a man by two women.

A Letter of Advice

(from Miss Medora Trevilian, at Padua, to Miss Araminta Vavasour, in London)

> Enfin, monsieur, un homme aimable;
> Voilà pourquoi je ne saurais l'aimer.—*Scribe.*

You tell me you're promised a lover,
  My own Araminta, next week;
Why cannot my fancy discover
  The hue of his coat and his cheek?
Alas! If he look like another,
  A vicar, a banker, a beau,
Be deaf to your father and mother,
  My own Araminta, say 'No!'

34

Miss Lane, at her Temple of Fashion,
   Taught us both how to sing and to speak,
And we loved one another with passion,
   Before we had been there a week:
You gave me a ring for a token;
   I wear it wherever I go;
I gave you a chain,—is it broken?
   My own Araminta, say 'No!'

O think of our favourite cottage,
   And think of our dear Lalla Rookh!
How we shared with the milkmaids their pottage,
   And drank of the stream from the brook:
How fondly our loving lips faltered
   'What further can grandeur bestow?'
My heart is the same;—is yours altered?
   My own Araminta, say 'No!'

Remember the thrilling romances
   We read on the bank in the glen;
Remember the suitors our fancies
   Would picture for both of us then.
They wore the red cross on their shoulder,
   They have vanquished and pardoned their foe—
Sweet friend, are you wiser or colder?
   My own Araminta, say 'No!'

You know, when Lord Rigmarole's carriage
   Drove off with your cousin Justine,
   You wept, dearest girl, at the marriage,
   And whispered 'How base she has been!'
You said you were sure it would kill you,
   If ever your husband looked so;
And you will not apostatize,—will you?
   My own Araminta, say 'No!'

When I heard I was going abroad, love,
    I thought I was going to die;
We walked arm in arm to the road, love,
    We looked arm in arm to the sky;
And I said 'When a foreign postilion
    Has hurried me off to the Po,
Forget not Medora Trevilian:
    My own Araminta, say "No!"'

We parted! but sympathy's fetters
    Reach far over valley and hill;
I muse o'er your exquisite letters,
    And feel that your heart is mine still;
And he who would share it with me, love,—
    The richest of treasures below—
If he's not what Orlando should be, love,
    My own Araminta, say 'No!'

If he wears a top-boot in his wooing,
    If he comes to you riding a cob,
If he talks of his baking or brewing,
    If he puts up his feet on the hob,
If he ever drinks port after dinner,
    If his brow or his breeding is low,
If he calls himself 'Thompson' or 'Skinner',
    My own Araminta, say 'No!'

If he studies the news in the papers
    While you are preparing the tea,
If he talks of the damps or the vapours
    While moonlight lies soft on the sea,
If he's sleepy while you are capricious,
    If he has not a musical 'Oh!'
If he does not call Werther delicious,—
    My own Araminta, say 'No!'

If he ever sets foot in the City
  Among the stockbrockers and Jews,
If he has not a heart full of pity,
  If he don't stand six feet in his shoes,
If his lips are not redder than roses,
  If his hands are not whiter than snow,
If he has not the model of noses,—
  My own Araminta, say 'No!'

If he speaks of a tax or a duty,
  If he does not look grand on his knees,
If he's blind to a landscape of beauty,
  Hills, valleys, rocks, waters and trees,
If he dotes not on desolate towers,
  If he likes not to hear the blast blow,
If he knows not the language of flowers,—
  My own Araminta, say 'No!'

He must walk—like a god of old story
  Come down from the home of his rest;
He must smile—like the sun in his glory
  On the buds he loves ever the best;
And oh! from its ivory portal
  Like music his soft speech must flow!—
If he speak, smile, or walk like a mortal,
  My own Araminta, say 'No!'

Don't listen to tales of his bounty,
  Don't hear what they say of his birth,
Don't look at his seat in the county,
  Don't calculate what he is worth;
But give him a theme to write verse on,
  And see if he turns out his toe;
If he's only an excellent person,—
  My own Araminta, say 'No!'

WINTHROP MACKWORTH PRAED

Varium et Mutabile

Is it possible
  That so high debate,
  So sharp, so sore, and of such rate,
  Should end so soon and was begun so late?
Is it possible?

Is it possible
  So cruel intent,
  So hasty heat and so soon spent,
  From love to hate, and thence for to relent?
Is it possible?

Is it possible
  That any may find
  Within one heart so diverse mind,
  To change or turn as weather and wind?
Is it possible?

Is it possible
  To spy it in an eye
  That turns as oft as chance on die,
  The truth whereof can any try?
Is it possible?

It is possible
  For to turn so oft,
  To bring that lowest that was most aloft,
  And to fall highest, yet to light soft.
It is possible.

All is possible,
  Who so list believe;
  Trust therefore first, and after preve,
  As men wed ladies by licence and leave,
All is possible.

SIR THOMAS WYATT

Anna Karenina

Levin, having once been refused, has been joyfully accepted by Kitty Shcherbatsky. This is his first visit after Kitty's acceptance.

It was past nine when he reached the Shcherbatskys' steps for the second time. The inmates of the house were only just up, and the cook came out to go marketing. Levin had to get through at least two hours more.

All that night and morning Levin had lived quite unconsciously, quite lifted out of the conditions of material existence. He had not eaten for a whole day, he had not slept for two nights, had spent several hours half-dressed and exposed to the frosty air, and he felt not only fresher and better than ever, but completely independent of his body: he moved without any effort of his muscles and felt capable of anything. He was sure he could fly upwards or lift the corner of a house, if need be. He spent the rest of the time walking about the streets, every other minute consulting his watch, and gazing about him.

And what he saw that morning, he never saw again. He was moved in particular by the children going to school, the silvery-grey pigeons that flew down from the roof to the pavement, and the little loaves of bread, powdered with flour, that some invisible hand had put outside a baker's shop. Those loaves, the pigeons, and the two little boys seemed not of this earth. It all happened at the same time: one of the boys ran towards a pigeon and looked smilingly up at Levin; the pigeon fluttered its wings and flew off, flashing in the sun amid the quivering snow-dust in the air, while from a little window came the smell of fresh-baked bread, and the loaves were put out. All this together was so extraordinarily nice that Levin laughed and cried with delight. After making a long round by Gazetny lane and Koslovka street, he returned to the hotel again, placed his watch before him, and sat down to wait for twelve o'clock. In the next room they were saying something about machines and fraud, and coughing as people do in the morning. They did not realize that the watch hand was nearing twelve. The hand reached twelve. Levin went out on to the steps. The cabmen evidently knew all about it. With happy faces they surrounded Levin, disputing among themselves and offering their services. He chose one, and not to offend the others promised to engage them some other time. He told the man to drive to the Shcherbatskys'. The sledge-driver looked charming with the white shirt-band sticking out over his coat and fitting tightly round his full, sturdy red neck. The sledge was high and comfortable, and never after did Levin drive in one like it, and the horse was a good one and tried its best to go fast but did not seem to move. The driver knew the Shcherbatsky's house, and rounding his elbows and calling 'Whoa!' in a manner especially indicative of respect for his fare drew up at the entrance. The Shcherbatskys' hall-porter certainly knew all about it. That was obvious from the smile in his eyes and the way he said:

'Well, it's a long time since you were here last, Constantine Dmitrich!'

Not only did he know all about it but he was unmistakably delighted, making efforts to conceal his joy. Glancing into his kindly old eyes, Levin felt something new even in his happiness.

'Are they up?'

'This way, sir! Leave it here, please,' said he, smiling, as Levin turned back for his fur cap. That meant something.

'To whom shall I announce you, sir?' a footman asked.

The footman, though a young man and one of the new school of footmen, a dandy, was very obliging and attentive, and he too understood the situation.

'The princess . . . I mean, the prince . . . the young princess . . .' said Levin.

The first person he saw was Mademoiselle Linon. She was passing through the hall and her ringlets and her face shone. He had barely exchanged a few words with her when he heard the rustle of a skirt at the door, and Mademoiselle Linon vanished from Levin's eyes, and his heart stood still at the nearness of his happiness. Mademoiselle Linon hurriedly left him and went towards the other door. Directly she had gone out, swift, swift light little steps sounded on the parquet, and his bliss, his life, his self—the better part of himself, which he had so long been seeking and hoping for—came rapidly towards him. She did not walk but was borne along by some invisible force.

He saw only her clear, truthful eyes, timid with the same bliss of love that flooded his own heart. Those eyes were shining nearer and nearer, dazzling him with their light of love. She stopped still close to him, touching him. She raised her arms and her hands dropped on to his shoulders.

She had done everything she could—she had run up to him and yielded herself entirely, shy and happy. He put his arms round her and pressed his lips to her mouth that sought his kiss.

She, too, had passed a sleepless night, and had been waiting for him all the morning.

Her mother and father had given their consent without demur, and were happy in her happiness. She had been on the watch for him. She wanted to be the first to tell him of her happiness and his. She had got ready to see him alone, and had rejoiced at the idea, and had felt shy and confused and had not known herself what she would do. She had heard his step and his voice, and had waited at the door for Mademoiselle Linon to go. Mademoiselle Linon had gone away. Without thinking, without asking herself how and what, she had gone up to him and acted in the way she had.

'Let us find Mama!' she said, taking him by the hand.

For a long while he could not speak, not so much because he was afraid that words might desecrate the loftiness of his emotion, as because every time he tried to say something he felt that, instead of words, tears of happiness would rush out. He took her hand and kissed it.

'Is it really true?' he said at last in a husky voice. 'I cannot believe you love me, dear!'

She smiled at that 'dear', and at the timidity with which he glanced at her.

'Yes!' she said significantly and slowly. 'I am so happy!'

Not letting go his hand, she entered the drawing-room. On seeing them the princess became rather breathless and immediately began to cry and then immediately began to laugh, and, running up to them with a vigorous step Levin had not expected, she took his head in both her hands and kissed him, wetting his cheeks with her tears.

'So it is all settled! I am glad. Love her. I am glad . . . Kitty!'

'You didn't take long arranging matters,' said the old prince, trying to appear indifferent; but Levin noticed that his eyes were moist when he turned to him.

'I have always hoped for this,' he said, taking Levin by the arm and drawing him towards himself. 'Even when this little feather-brain thought of . . .'

'Papa!' cried Kitty, and shut his mouth with her hands.

'All right, I won't!' he said. 'I am very, very . . . plea . . . Oh, what a fool I am . . .!'

He took Kitty in his arms, kissed her face, her hand, her face again, and made the sign of the cross over her.

And Levin was seized with a new feeling of affection for this old man, who had been a stranger to him before, when he saw how fervently and tenderly Kitty kissed his strong hand.

The princess was sitting in her arm-chair, silent and smiling; the prince seated himself beside her. Kitty stood by her father's chair, still holding his hand. No one spoke.

The princess was the first to put everything into words, and bring all their thoughts and feelings back to the practical side of life. And for a moment this seemed strange and even painful to them all.

'When is it to be? We must have the betrothal and announce it. And when's the wedding to be? What do you think, Alexander?'

'There's the hero,' said the old prince, pointing to Levin. 'He's the principal person concerned.'

'When?' said Levin, blushing. 'To-morrow. If you ask me, I should say, the betrothal to-day and the wedding to-morrow.'

'Come now, *mon cher*, that's nonsense!'

'Well then, next week.'

'He's quite mad.'

'Why not?'

'Upon my word!' said the mother, with a pleased smile at this haste. 'And how about the trousseau?'

'Must there really be a trousseau and all that?' Levin thought with horror. 'However . . . as if a trousseau and a betrothal ceremony and the rest could spoil my happiness! Nothing can spoil it!' He glanced at Kitty, and noticed that she was not in the least, not in the very least, disturbed at the idea of a trousseau. 'Then it must be necessary,' he thought.

'Oh, I know nothing about it; I only said what I should like,' he said apologetically.

'We'll talk it over, then. We can have the betrothal now and make the announcement. That will be all right.'

The princess went up to her husband, kissed him, and was about to go away, but he stopped her, put his arm round her and tenderly, like a young lover, kissed her several times, smiling. The two old people were evidently confused for a moment, and did not quite know whether it was they who were in love again or only their daughter. When the prince and princess had gone, Levin went up to his betrothed and took her hand. He had now regained his self-possession and could speak, and there was much he had to say to her. But what he said was not at all what he had intended.

'How well I knew it would happen! I never dared hope, yet at the bottom of my heart I was always certain,' he said. 'I believe it was pre-ordained.'

'And I!' she said. 'Even when . . .' She stopped and went on again, looking at him resolutely with those truthful eyes of hers, '. . . even when I drove my happiness from me. I never loved anyone except you, but I was carried away. I must ask you: can you forget it?'

'Perhaps it was for the best. You have much to forgive me. I ought to tell you . . .'

This was one of the things he had made up his mind to speak about. He had resolved from the first to tell her two things—that he was not chaste as she was, and that he was an agnostic. It was agonizing, but he considered he ought to tell her both these facts.

'No, not now, later!' he said.

'All right, later, but you must certainly tell me. I'm not afraid of anything. I want to know everything. Now it is settled.'

He finished the sentence. 'Settled that you'll take me whatever I may be—you won't go back on your word, will you?'

'Oh no!'

They were interrupted by Mademoiselle Linon, who with an artificial but affectionate smile came to congratulate her favourite pupil. Before she had gone, the servants came in with their congratulations. Then relations arrived, and there began that blissful hubbub which went on until the day after the wedding. Levin continually felt uncomfortable and awkward but the intensity of his happiness kept increasing all the while. He felt all the time that a great deal was being expected of him—what, he did not know; and he did everything he was told, and it all gave him joy. He had thought his courtship would have nothing in common with other courtships, that the ordinary conditions of engaged couples would spoil his peculiar happiness; but it ended in his doing exactly as other people did, and his happiness was thereby only increased, becoming more and more personal and unlike anyone else's ever was.

'Now we shall have bonbons to eat,' Mademoiselle Linon happened to say, and off Levin went to buy bonbons.

'Well, I'm very glad,' said Sviazhsky. 'I advise you to go to Fomin's for the flowers.'

'Oh, are they wanted?' And he drove to Fomin's.

His brother told him he ought to borrow money, as there would be a great many expenses, presents to give . . .

'Oh, are presents wanted?' And he galloped to buy jewellery at Foulde's.

And at the confectioner's, and at Fomin's, and at Foulde's he saw that he was expected, that they were pleased to see him and rejoiced in his happiness, just like everyone else with whom he had to do during those days. What was extraordinary was that everyone not only liked him but even people who had formerly been unfriendly, cold, or indifferent now delighted in him, gave way to him in everything, treated his feelings with delicate consideration, and shared his conviction that he was the happiest man on earth because his betrothed was the height of perfection. Kitty, too, felt the same thing. When the Countess Nordston ventured to hint that she had hoped for something better, Kitty got so heated and proved so conclusively that nothing ιn the world could be better than Levin that Countess Nordston h ad to admit it, and thereafter in Kitty's presence never failed to greet Levin with a smile of ecstatic admiration.

LEO TOLSTOY

From A Letter

I like not only to be loved but also to be told that I am loved. The realm of silence is large enough beyond the grave. This is the world of light and speech. And I shall take leave to tell you that you are very dear.

GEORGE ELIOT

Youth and Cupid

When I was fair and young, and favour graced me,
    Of many was I sought, their mistress for to be;
But I did scorn them all, and answered them therefore,
    'Go, go, go, seek some otherwhere,
      Importune me no more!'

How many weeping eyes I made to pine with woe,
    How many sighing hearts, I have no skill to show;
Yet I the prouder grew, and answered them therefore,
    'Go, go, go, seek some otherwhere,
      Importune me no more!'

Then spake fair Venus' son, that proud victorious boy,
    And said: 'Fine dame, since that you be so coy,
I will so pluck your plumes that you shall say no more,
    'Go, go, go, seek some otherwhere,
      Importune me no more!'

When he had spake these words, such change grew
      in my breast
That neither night nor day since that, I could take
      any rest.
Then lo! I did repent that I had said before,
    'Go, go, go, seek some otherwhere,
      Importune me no more!'

QUEEN ELIZABETH I

Stendhal to Madame Curial

           Paris, Tuesday evening, 18 May, 1824
What a sad thing adversity is, or at least how sad it makes me!
I was the happiest of men or at least my heart was beating with
powerful feelings when I went to your house this morning, and

these feelings were sweet indeed. I spent the evening and almost the whole day with you, but with such a show of indifference that I must make an effort to convince myself that things could be otherwise. For the first time in ten years I regret having forgotten the practices of French society.

How can I see you? When will it be convenient for me to present myself again at your house? I did not go there yesterday, because a servant had seen me the day before asking the porter if you were at home. Are you satisfied with my discretion? Did I appear sufficiently unconcerned? I am angry with myself at the thought of it. For pity's sake let me know by letter the exact moments when I shall be able to find you alone. Foregoing these moments is the furthest thing from my mind at present, and I despair of ever seeing you alone in view of the number of visits which you receive.

A small signal at the window of the boudoir where you were this morning, for example, a half-closed shutter or a half-lowered blind, would tell me that I could come up. If I do not see this sign that you are alone I shall refrain from knocking on the door and will try again a quarter of an hour later.

Must it be that you will leave without my seeing you?

Anonymous Suicide Note (Twentieth Century)

No wish to die. One of the best of sports, which they all knew. Not in the wrong, the boys will tell you. This b---- at Palmer's Green has sneaked my wife, one of the best in the world; my wife, the first love in the world.

Roman De La Rose

A piece from a prose translation of this Allegory of Love, written about the middle of the thirteenth century.

Now the God of Love came up to me, calling for my surrender; and this I could not refuse, but asked only that one day he would have mercy on me. I wished to kiss his feet, but he took me by the hand saying:

'From this you gain greatly, for I wish you here and now to do me homage to your own advantage. You will kiss me on the mouth, a favour I would grant to no base or uncouth fellow: only courtly and noble men do I take in this way as my vassals. Those who serve me have certainly to endure great toil and tribulation; but I do you great honour, and you should rejoice to have so good a master, so renowned a lord, who bears Love's standard and the banner of Courtesy: so gentle, upright and noble is he that whoever serves and honours him with zeal rejects baseness, wrongful deeds and all bad influence.' Then I became his man, hands joined in his; and you can imagine how my heart leapt when his mouth kissed mine.

The God then demanded some gage of my fidelity. 'Sire,' I said, 'you have taken possession of my heart. Put a lock on it, then, and take away the key.' To this he consented, and with a tiny golden key locked my heart so gently that I scarcely felt his touch. He told me that if I was loyal, patient and prepared to suffer, he would advance me far. Then he made his commandments.

I must avoid baseness and telling what should be concealed, be discreet and fair of speech, honour and serve all women and guard against pride. I must cultivate cleanliness and elegance in dress, be gay and ready to show off my particular skills, and gain a reputation for generosity.

'Now I order you as a penance to fix your every thought on love, night and day, without remission; think of it always, ceaselessly, bearing in mind that sweet moment whose joy is so long delayed And so that you may be a noble lover, I wish and command you to have your whole heart in a single place, so that it is not divided but quite entire, without deceit, since I have no liking for duplicity. . . . Take care not to lend it out, a wretched act in my eyes; but surrender it as an outright gift, and the greater merit will be yours. . . .

When you have given your heart as I have told you, there will be hard and cruel trials for you to undergo. Often, when your love comes to your mind, you will be forced to leave people's company so they may not see the trouble that racks you. You will keep yourself to yourself, sighing, lamenting, trembling and more besides, suffering in many ways: now hot, now cold, flushed one moment, pale another; no steady or recurring fever is so distressing. Before you escape you will have sampled all the pains of love. Frequently your thoughts will make you oblivious to all else, and for a long time you will be like a mute statue, still and motionless, not stirring a foot or a finger, hands or eyes, quite without speech. At length you will come to your senses again and, startled to do so, will tremble like a man afraid. Then you will heave deep sighs; for this, to be sure, is what those people do who have known the ills that so afflict you now.'

He told me I would go in search of my beloved; and, if I found her, her beauty would kindle my passion all the more, though courage to address her would fail me, for only false lovers chatter freely. At night I would toss and turn, think she was in my arms, then, finding myself deceived, lament aloud and pray for the dawn to come and end my misery. How, I asked, can lovers endure all these ills? The God answered that Hope would be my chief protector, while Fair Thought, Fair Speech and Fair Glance would also stand me in good stead. With that, he suddenly disappeared.

GUILLAUME DE LORRIS

The Baite

Come live with mee, and bee my love,
And wee will some new pleasures prove
Of golden sands, and christall brookes,
With silken lines, and silver hookes.

There will the river whispering runne
Warm'd by thy eyes, more than the Sunne.
And there the'inamor'd fish will stay,
Begging themselves they may betray.

When thou wilt swimme in that live bath,
Each fish, which every channell hath,
Will amorously to thee swimme,
Gladder to catch thee, than thou him.

48

If thou, to be so seene, beest loath,
By Sunne, or Moone, thou darknest both,
And if my selfe have lea✓e to see,
I need not their light, having thee.

Let others freeze with angling reeds,
And cut their legges, with shells and weeds,
Or treacherously poore fish beset,
With strangling snare, or windowie net:

Let coarse bold hands, from slimy nest
The bedded fish in banks out-west,
Or curious traitors, sleavesilke flies
Bewitch poore fishes wandring eyes.

For thee, thou needst no such deceit,
For thou thy selfe art thine owne bait;
That fish, that is not catch'd thereby,
Alas, is wiser farre than I.

JOHN DONNE

Pride and Prejudice

*Here is Mr Darcy's first declaration of love to Elizabeth
Bennet. For those who may not know it—these two characters
impersonate the title of the novel.*

When they were gone, Elizabeth, as if intending to exasperate
herself as much as possible against Mr Darcy, chose for her
employment the examination of all the letters which Jane had
written to her since her being in Kent. They contained no actual
complaint, nor was there any revival of past occurrences, or any
communication of present suffering. But in all, and in almost every
line of each, there was a want of that cheerfulness which had been
used to characterise her style, and which, proceeding from the
serenity of a mind at ease with itself, and kindly disposed towards
every one, had been scarcely ever clouded. Elizabeth noticed

every sentence conveying the idea of uneasiness, with an attention which it had hardly received on the first perusal. Mr Darcy's shameful boast of what misery he had been able to inflict gave her a keener sense of her sister's sufferings. It was some consolation to think that his visit to Rosings was to end on the day after the next, and a still greater that in less than a fortnight she should herself be with Jane again, and enabled to contribute to the recovery of her spirits, by all that affection could do.

She could not think of Darcy's leaving Kent without remembering that his cousin was to go with him; but Colonel Fitzwilliam had made it clear that he had no intentions at all, and, agreeable as he was, she did not mean to be unhappy about him.

While settling this point, she was suddenly roused by the sound of the door bell; and her spirits were a little fluttered by the idea of its being Colonel Fitzwilliam himself, who had once before called late in the evening, and might now come to inquire particularly after her. But this idea was soon banished, and her spirits were very differently affected, when, to her utter amazement, she saw Mr Darcy walk into the room. In a hurried manner he immediately began an inquiry after her health, imputing his visit to a wish of hearing that she were better. She answered him with cold civility. He sat down for a few moments, and then getting up, walked about the room. Elizabeth was surprised, but said not a word. After a silence of several minutes, he came towards her in an agitated manner, and thus began:—

'In vain have I struggled. It will not do. My feelings will not be repressed. You must allow me to tell you how ardently I admire and love you.'

Elizabeth's astonishment was beyond expression. She stared, coloured, doubted, and was silent. This he considered sufficient encouragement, and the avowal of all that he felt and had long felt for her immediately followed. He spoke well, but there were feelings besides those of the heart to be detailed, and he was not more eloquent on the subject of tenderness than of pride. His sense of her inferiority, of its being a degradation, of the family obstacles which judgment had always opposed to inclination, were dwelt on with a warmth which seemed due to the consequence he was wounding, but was very unlikely to recommend his suit.

In spite of her deeply-rooted dislike, she could not be insensible to the compliment of such a man's affection, and though her intentions did not vary for an instant, she was at first sorry for the pain he was to receive; till, roused to resentment by his subsequent language, she lost all compassion in anger. She tried, however, to compose herself to answer him with patience, when he should have done. He concluded with representing to her the strength of that attachment which, in spite of all his endeavours, he had found impossible to conquer; and with expressing his hope that it would now be rewarded by her acceptance of his hand. As he said this she could easily see that he had no doubt of a favourable answer. He *spoke* of apprehension and anxiety, but his countenance expressed real security. Such a circumstance could only exasperate farther; and when he ceased the colour rose into her cheeks and she said,—

'In such cases as this, it is, I believe, the established mode to express a sense of obligation for the sentiments avowed, however unequally they may be returned. It is natural that obligation should be felt, and if I could *feel* gratitude, I would now thank you. But I cannot—I have never desired your good opinion, and you have certainly bestowed it most unwillingly. I am sorry to have occasioned pain to any one. It has been most unconsciously done, however, and I hope will be of short duration. The feelings which you tell me have long prevented the acknowledgement of your regard can have little difficulty in overcoming it after this explanation.'

Mr Darcy, who was leaning against the mantelpiece with his eyes fixed on her face, seemed to catch her words with no less resentment than surprise. His complexion became pale with anger, and the disturbance of his mind was visible in every feature. He was struggling for the appearance of composure, and would not open his lips till he believed himself to have attained it. The pause was to Elizabeth's feelings dreadful. At length, in a voice of forced calmness, he said,—

'And this is all the reply which I am to have the honour of expecting! I might, perhaps, wish to be informed why, with so little *endeavour* at civility, I am thus rejected. But it is of small importance.'

'I might as well inquire,' replied she, 'why, with so evident a design of offending and insulting me, you chose to tell me that you liked me against your will, against your reason, and even against your character? Was not this some excuse for incivility, if I *was* uncivil? But I have other provocations. You know I have.

Had not my own feelings decided against you, had they been indifferent, or had they even been favourable, do you think that any consideration would tempt me to accept the man who has been the means of ruining, perhaps for ever, the happiness of a most beloved sister?'

As she pronounced these words, Mr Darcy changed colour; but the emotion was short, and he listened without attempting to interrupt her while she continued,—

'I have every reason in the world to think ill of you. No motive can excuse the unjust and ungenerous part you acted *there*. You dare not, you cannot, deny that you have been the principal, if not the only means of dividing them from each other, of exposing one to the censure of the world for caprice and instability, the other to its derision for disappointed hopes, and involving them both in misery of the acutest kind.'

She paused, and saw with no slight indignation that he was listening with an air which proved him wholly unmoved by any feeling of remorse. He even looked at her with a smile of affected incredulity.

'Can you deny that you have done it?' she repeated.

With assumed tranquillity he then replied, 'I have no wish of denying that I did everything in my power to separate my friend from your sister, or that I rejoice in my success. Towards *him* I have been kinder than towards myself.'

Elizabeth disdained the appearance of noticing this civil reflection, but its meaning did not escape, nor was it likely to conciliate her.

'But it is not merely this affair,' she continued, 'on which my dislike is founded. Long before it had taken place, my opinion of you was decided. Your character was unfolded in the recital which I received many months ago from Mr Wickham. On this subject, what can you have to say? In what imaginary act of friendship can you here defend yourself? or under what mis-representation can you here impose upon others?'

'You take an eager interest in that gentleman's concerns,' said Darcy, in a less tranquil tone, and with a heightened colour.

'Who that knows what his misfortunes have been can help feeling an interest in him?'

'His misfortunes!' repeated Darcy, contemptuously,—'yes, his misfortunes have been great indeed.'

'And of your infliction,' cried Elizabeth, with energy. 'You have reduced him to his present state of poverty—comparative poverty. You have withheld the advantages which you must know to have been designed for him. You have deprived the best years of his life of that independence which was no less his due than his desert. You have done all this! and yet you can treat the mention of his misfortunes with contempt and ridicule.'

'And this,' cried Darcy, as he walked with quick steps across the room, 'is your opinion of me! This is the estimation in which you hold me! I thank you for explaining it so fully. My faults, according to this calculation, are heavy indeed! But, perhaps,' added he, stopping in his walk, and turning towards her, 'these offences might have been overlooked, had not your pride been hurt by my honest confession of the scruples that had long prevented my forming any serious design. These bitter accusations might have been suppressed, had I, with greater policy, concealed my struggles, and flattered you into the belief of my being impelled by unqualified, unalloyed inclination; by reason, by reflection, by everything. But disguise of every sort is my abhorrence. Nor am I ashamed of the feelings I related. They were natural and just. Could you expect me to rejoice in the inferiority of your connections? To congratulate myself on the hope of relations whose condition in life is so decidedly beneath my own?'

Elizabeth felt herself growing more angry every moment; yet she tried to the utmost to speak with composure when she said,—

'You are mistaken, Mr Darcy, if you suppose that the mode of your declaration affected me in any other way than as it spared me the concern which I might have felt in refusing you, had you behaved in a more gentlemanlike manner.'

She saw him start at this; but he said nothing, and she continued,—

'You could not have made me the offer of your hand in any possible way that would have tempted me to accept it.'

Again his astonishment was obvious; and he looked at her with an expression of mingled incredulity and mortification. She went on,—

'From the very beginning, from the first moment, I may almost say, of my acquaintance with you, your manners, impressing me with the fullest belief of your arrogance, your conceit, and your selfish disdain of the feelings of others, were such as to form that groundwork of disapprobation on which succeeding events have built so immovable a dislike; and I had not known you a month before I felt that you were the last man in the world whom I could ever be prevailed on to marry.'

'You have said quite enough, madam. I perfectly comprehend your feelings, and have now only to be ashamed of what my own have been. Forgive me for having taken up so much of your time, and accept my best wishes for your health and happiness.'

And with these words he hastily left the room, and Elizabeth heard him the next moment open the front door and quit the house. The tumult of her mind was now painfully great. She knew not how to support herself, and, from actual weakness, sat down and cried for half an hour. Her astonishment, as she reflected on what had passed, was increased by every review of it. That she should receive an offer of marriage from Mr Darcy! that he should have been in love with her for so many months! so much in love as to wish to marry her in spite of all the objections which had made him prevent his friend's marrying her sister, and which must appear at least with equal force in his own case, was almost incredible! it was gratifying to have inspired unconsciously so strong an affection. But his pride, his abominable pride, his shameless avowal of what he had done with respect to Jane, his unpardonable assurance in acknowledging, though he could not justify it, and the unfeeling manner in which he had mentioned Mr Wickham, his cruelty towards whom he had not attempted to deny, soon overcame the pity which the consideration of his attachment had for a moment excited.

She continued in very agitating reflections till the sound of Lady Catherine's carriage made her feel how unequal she was to encounter Charlotte's observation, and hurried her away to her room.

Here is Mr Darcy's second proposal.

Instead of receiving any such letter of excuse from his friend as Elizabeth half expected Mr Bingley to do, he was able to bring Darcy with him to Longbourn before many days had passed after Lady Catherine's visit. The gentlemen arrived early; and, before Mrs Bennet had time to tell him of their having seen his aunt, of which her daughter sat in momentary dread, Bingley, who wanted to be alone with Jane, proposed their all walking out. It was agreed to. Mrs Bennet was not in the habit of walking, Mary could never spare time, but the remaining five set off together. Bingley and Jane, however, soon allowed the others to outstrip them. They lagged behind, while Elizabeth, Kitty, and Darcy were to entertain each other. Very little was said by either; Kitty was too much afraid of him to talk; Elizabeth was secretly forming a desperate resolution; and, perhaps, he might be doing the same.

They walked towards the Lucases', because Kitty wished to call upon Maria; and as Elizabeth saw no occasion for making it a general concern, when Kitty left them she went boldly on with him alone. Now was the moment for her resolution to be executed; and while her courage was high she immediately said,—

'Mr Darcy, I am a very selfish creature, and for the sake of giving relief to my own feelings care not how much I may be wounding yours. I can no longer help thanking you for your unexampled kindness to my poor sister. Ever since I have known it I have been most anxious to acknowledge to you how gratefully I feel it. Were it known to the rest of my family I should not have merely my own gratitude to express.'

'I am sorry, exceedingly sorry,' replied Darcy, in a tone of surprise and emotion, 'that you have ever been informed of what may, in a mistaken light, have given you uneasiness. I did not think Mrs Gardiner was so little to be trusted.'

'You must not blame my aunt. Lydia's thoughtlessness first betrayed to me that you had been concerned in the matter; and, of course, I could not rest till I knew the particulars. Let me thank you again and again, in the name of all my family, for that generous compassion which induced you to take so much trouble, and bear so many mortifications, for the sake of discovering them.'

'If you *will* thank me,' he replied, 'let it be for yourself alone. That the wish of giving happiness to you might add force to the other inducements which led me on I shall not attempt to deny. But your *family* owe me nothing. Much as I respect them, I believe I thought only of *you*.'

Elizabeth was too much embarrassed to say a word. After a short pause, her companion added, 'You are too generous to trifle with me. If your feelings are still what they were last April, tell me so at once. *My* affections and wishes are unchanged; but one word from you will silence me on this subject for ever.'

Elizabeth, feeling all the more than common awkwardness and anxiety for his situation, now forced herself to speak; and immediately, though not very fluently, gave him to understand that her sentiments had undergone so material a change since the period to which he alluded as to make her receive with gratitude and pleasure his present assurances. The happiness which this reply produced was such as he had probably never felt before; and he expressed himself on the occasion as sensibly and as warmly as a man violently in love can be supposed to do. Had Elizabeth been able to encounter his eyes, she might have seen how well the expression of heartfelt delight, diffused over his face, became him; but though she could not look she could listen; and he told her of feelings which, in proving of what importance she was to him, made his affection every moment more valuable.

They walked on without knowing in what direction.

. . . .

JANE AUSTEN

A Description of Love

Now what is love? I pray thee, tell.
It is that fountain and that well,
Where pleasure and repentance dwell.
It is perhaps that sauncing bell,
That tolls all in to heaven or hell:
And this is love, as I hear tell.

Yet what is love? I pray thee say.
It is a work on holy-day;
It is December matched with May;
When lusty bloods, in fresh array,
Hear ten months after of the play:
And this is love, as I hear say.

Yet what is love? I pray thee sayn.
It is a sunshine mixed with rain;
It is a tooth-ache, or like pain;
It is a game where none doth gain;
The lass saith no, and would full fain:
And this is love, as I hear sayn.

Yet what is love? I pray thee say.
It is a yea, it is a nay,
A pretty kind of sporting fray;
It is a thing will soon away;
Then take the vantage while you may:
And this is love, as I hear say.

Yet what is love? I pray thee show.
A thing that creeps, it cannot go;
A prize that passeth to and fro;
A thing for one, a thing for mo;
And he that proves must find it so:
And this is love, sweet friend, I trow.

SIR WALTER RALEGH

sauncing: sacring, at mass

James Joyce to Nora Barnacle

60 Shelbourne Road
15 August 1904

My dear Nora,

It has just struck me. I came in at half past eleven. Since then I have been sitting in an easy chair like a fool. I could do nothing. I hear nothing but your voice. I am like a fool hearing you call me 'Dear.' I offended two men today by leaving them coolly. I wanted to hear your voice, not theirs.

When I am with you I leave aside my contemptuous, suspicious nature. I wish I felt your head on my shoulder. I think I will go to bed.

I have been a half-hour writing this thing. Will you write something to me? I hope you will. How am I to sign myself? I won't sign anything at all, because I don't know what to sign myself.

King Henry VIII to Anne Boleyn (1528)

My mistress and friend,

I and my heart put ourselves in your hands, begging you to recommend us to your good grace and not to let absence lessen your affection, for it were great pity to increase their pain, seeing that absence does that sufficiently and more than I could ever have thought possible; reminding us of a point in astronomy, which is that the longer the days are the farther off is the sun and yet the hotter; so is it with our love, for although by absence we are parted it nevertheless keeps its fervency, at least in my case and hoping the like of yours; assuring you that for myself the pang of absence is already too great, and when I think of the increase of what I must needs suffer it would be well nigh intolerable but for my firm hope of your unchangeable affection; and sometimes to put you in mind of this, and seeing that in person I cannot be with you, I send you now something most nearly pertaining thereto that is at present possible to send, that is to say, my picture set in a bracelet with the whole device which you already know; wishing myself in their place when it shall please you. This by the hand of

Your loyal servant and friend,

H Rex

Henry VIII to Anne Boleyn

Mine own sweetheart, this shall be to advertise you of the great elengeness that I find here since your departing; for I ensure you methinketh the time longer since your departing now last than I was wont to do a whole fortnight. I think your kindness and my fervency of love causeth it; for otherwise I would not have thought it possible that for so little a while it should have grieved me. But now that I am coming towards you, methinketh my pains be half released, and also I am right well comforted in so much that my book maketh substantially for my matter; in looking whereof I have spent above four hours this day, which caused me now to write the shorter letter to you at this time, because of some pain in my head; wishing myself (specially an evening) in my sweetheart's arms, whose pretty dukkys I trust shortly to cusse.

Written with the hand of him that was, is, and shall be yours by his will,

H.R.

King Henry VIII to Anne Boleyn [c. 1528]

In debating with myself the contents of your letters I have been put to a great agony; not knowing how to understand them, whether to my disadvantage as shown in some places, or to my advantage as in others. I beseech you now with all my heart definitely to let me know your whole mind as to the love between us; for necessity compels me to plague you for a reply, having been for more than a year now struck by the dart of love, and being uncertain either of failure or of finding a place in your heart and affection, which point has certainly kept me for some time from naming you my mistress, since if you only love me with an ordinary love the name is not appropriate to you, seeing that it stands for an uncommon position very remote from the ordinary; but if it pleases you to do the duty of a true, loyal mistress and friend, and to give yourself body and heart to me, who have been, and will be, your very loyal servant (if your rigour does not forbid me), I promise you that not only the name will be due to you, but also to take you as my sole mistress, casting off all others than yourself out of mind and affection, and to serve you only; begging you to make me a complete reply to this my rude letter as to how far and in what I can trust; and if it does not please you to reply in writing, to let me know of some place where I can have it by word of mouth, the which place I will seek out with all my heart. No more for fear of wearying you. Written by the hand of him who would willingly remain your

HR

Lines supposed to have been addressed to
Fanny Brawne

This living hand, now warm and capable
Of earnest grasping, would, if it were cold
And in the icy silence of the tomb,
So haunt thy days and chill thy dreaming nights
That thou would[st] wish thine own heart dry of blood
So in my veins red life might stream again,
And thou be conscience-calm'd—see here it is—
I hold it towards you.

JOHN KEATS

Modern Love

And what is Love? It is a doll, dressed up
For idleness to cosset, nurse and dandle;
A thing of soft misnomers, so divine
That silly youth doth think to make itself
Divine by loving, and so goes on
Yawning and doting a whole summer long,
Till Miss's comb is made a pearl tiara,
And common Wellingtons turn Romeo boots;
Then Cleopatra lives at number seven,
And Antony resides in Brunswick Square.
Fools! if some passions high have warmed the world,
If Queens and Soldiers have played deep for hearts,
It is no reason why such agonies
Should be more common than the growth of weeds.
Fools! make me whole again that weighty pearl
The Queen of Egypt melted, and I'll say
That ye may love in spite of beaver hats.

JOHN KEATS

To Miss Fanny Brawne

My dearest Girl,

   This moment I have set myself to copy some verses out fair. I cannot proceed with any degree of content. I must write you a line or two and see if that will assist in dismissing you from my Mind for ever so short a time. Upon my Soul I can think of nothing else. The time is passed when I had power to advise and warn you against the unpromising morning of my Life. My love has made me selfish. I cannot exist without you. I am forgetful of everything but seeing you again—my Life seems to stop there—I see no further. You have absorb'd me. I have a sensation at the present moment as though I was dissolving—I should be exquisitely miserable without the hope of soon seeing you. I should be afraid to separate myself far from you. My sweet Fanny, will your heart never change? My love, will it? I have no limit now to my love. . . . Your note came in just here. I cannot be happier away from you. 'Tis richer than an Argosy of Pearles. Do not threat me even in jest. I have been astonished that Men could die Martyrs for religion—I have shudder'd at it. I shudder no more—I could be martyr'd for my Religion—Love is my religion—I could die for that. I could die for you. My Creed is Love and you are its only tenet. You have ravish'd me away by a Power I cannot resist; and yet I could resist till I saw you; and even since I have seen you I have endeavoured often 'to reason against the reasons of my Love'. I can do that no more—the pain would be too great. My love is selfish. I cannot breathe without you.

Yours for ever,

John Keats.

The Passionate Shepherd to his Love

Come live with me and be my love,
And we will all the pleasures prove,
That hills and valleys, dales and fields,
And all the craggy mountains yields.

There we will sit upon the rocks,
And see the shepherds feed their flocks,
By shallow rivers to whose falls
Melodious birds sing madrigals.

And I will make thee beds of roses
With a thousand fragrant posies,
A cap of flowers, and a kirtle
Embroidered all with leaves of myrtle;

A gown made of the finest wool
Which from our pretty lambs we pull;
Fair lined slippers for the cold,
With buckles of the purest gold;

A belt of straw and ivy buds,
With coral clasps and amber studs:
And if these pleasures may thee move,
Come live with me and be my love.

The shepherds' swains shall dance and sing
For thy delight each May morning:
If these delights thy mind may move,
Then live with me and be my love.

CHRISTOPHER MARLOWE

Answer to Marlowe

If all the world and love were young,
And truth in every shepherd's tongue,
These pretty pleasures might me move
To live with thee and be thy love.

Time drives the flocks from field to fold,
When rivers rage and rocks grow cold,
And Philomel becometh dumb;
The rest complain of cares to come.

The flowers do fade, and wanton fields
To wayward winter reckoning yields;
A honey tongue, a heart of gall,
Is fancy's spring, but sorrow's fall.

Thy gowns, thy shoes, thy beds of roses,
Thy cap, thy kirtle, and thy posies
Soon break, soon wither, soon forgotten,
In folly ripe, in reason rotten.

Thy belt of straw and ivy buds,
Thy coral clasps and amber studs,
All these in me no means can move
To come to thee and be thy love.

But could youth last and love still breed,
Had joys no date nor age no need,
Then these delights my mind might move
To live with thee and be thy love.

SIR WALTER RALEGH

Frederic Chopin to Delphine Potocka

Fidelina, my one and only beloved:
   I will bore you once again with my thoughts on the subject of inspiration and creativity, but as you will perceive these thoughts are directly connected with you.
   I have long reflected on inspiration and creativity and slowly, slowly I think I have discovered the essential nature of these gifts.
   To me inspiration and creativity come only when I have abstained from a woman for a longish period. When, with passion, I have emptied my fluid into a woman until I am pumped dry then

inspiration shuns me and ideas won't crawl into my head. Consider how strange and wonderful it is that the same forces which go to fertilise a woman and create a human being should go to create a work of art! Yet a man wastes this life-giving precious fluid for a moment of ecstasy.

The same is true of scholars who devote themselves to scientific pursuits or men who make discoveries. The formula is apparently a simple one: whatever the field, the creator must abjure woman—then the forces in his body will accumulate in his brain in the form of inspiration and he may give birth to a pure work of art.

Just think of it—sexual temptation and desire can be transmitted into inspiration! Of course I am speaking only of those who have ability and talent. A fool, living without a woman, will merely be driven insane by frustration. He can't create anything worthy of God or man.

On the other hand unrequited love and unfulfilled passion, sharpened by the image of one's beloved and carrying unbearable frustration with it, can contribute to creativity. I have observed this in Norwid (a Polish poet).

What about Mozart? I don't know, but I think his wife became ordinary food for him, his love and passion cooled, and he therefore was able to compose a great deal. I haven't heard of love-affairs in Mozart's life.

Sweetest Fidelina, how much of that precious fluid, how many forces have I wasted on you! I have not given you a child and God only knows how many excellent inspirations, how many musical ideas have gone to perdition!

Operam et oleunsa perdidi (I wasted the work and the labour) !!! Who knows what ballades, polonaises, perhaps an entire concerto, have been forever engulfed in your little D flat major. I cannot reckon what might have been, since I have not composed anything for ever so long, immersed as I was in you and in love. Works which could have come to life, drowned in your sweetest little D flat major, so that you are filled with music and pregnant with my compositions!

Time flies, life runs on, no one can recapture wasted moments. It is with reason that the saints call woman the gate to hell!

No, no I take back this last sentence. I eat my words. I won't erase what I have just written because if I do so you'll bother me until I tell you what the erased words were. And I don't have time to write another letter.

To me you are the gate of paradise. For you I will renounce fame, creativity, everything. Fidelina, Fidelina—I long for you intensely and frightfully.

I'm shivering as if ants were running up my spine to my head. When you finally arrive in your diligence I will glue myself to you, so that for a whole week you wont be able to tear me away from the little D flat major, and to hell with inspiration and ideas. Let my composition disappear in the dark forever.

Ah! I have thought up a new musical name for the little D flat major. Shall we call it 'tacit' (expressed in musical notation by—). I'll explain it to you at once: isn't a pause a hole in the melody? So this name is a musical term quite appropriate for the little D flat major.

Hoffmann just came and scattered to the wind the possibility of writing a letter. The pupils will shortly arrive as well, I will therefore finish, so that my letter can leave by today's mail. I kiss your beloved little body all over.

> Your most faithful Frederic
> Your entirely faithful Frederic
> Your *most* gifted pupil, one who has
> skilfully mastered the art of making love

P.S. I wasted time doing nothing yesterday and the letter did not leave, so I am adding to it.
I have just finished a Prelude.

The Olympic Girl

The sort of girl I like to see
Smiles down from her great height at me.
She stands in strong, athletic pose
And wrinkles her *retroussé* nose.
Is it distaste that makes her frown,

65

So furious and freckled, down
On an unhealthy worm like me?
Or am I what she likes to see?
I do not know, though much I care.
ειθε γενοιμην . . . would I were
(Forgive me, shade of Rupert Brooke)
An object fit to claim her look.
Oh! would I were her racket press'd
With hard excitement to her breast
And swished into the sunlit air
Arm-high above her tousled hair,
And banged against the bounding ball
'Oh! Plung!' my tauten'd strings would call,
'Oh! Plung! my darling, break my strings
For you I will do brilliant things.'
And when the match is over, I
Would flop beside you, hear you sigh;
And then, with what supreme caress,
You'ld tuck me up into my press.
Fair tigress of the tennis courts,
So short in sleeve and strong in shorts,
Little, alas, to you I mean,
For I am bald and old and green.

JOHN BETJEMAN

Feste's Song

O Mistress mine, where are you roaming?
O! stay and hear; your true love's coming,
   That can sing both high and low.
Trip no further, pretty sweeting;
Journeys end in lovers meeting,
   Every wise man's son doth know.

What is love? 'Tis not hereafter;
Present mirth hath present laughter;
　　What's to come is still unsure.
In delay there lies no plenty;
Then come kiss me, sweet and twenty;
　　Youth's a stuff will not endure.

WILLIAM SHAKESPEARE

The Woodlanders

Marty and Grace have always loved Giles, but Grace married the faithless Dr Fitzpiers who has left her. Giles has died of exposure through saving her honour and both girls have a weekly tryst to lay flowers on his grave. Grace meets Fitzpiers one night and does not return home. An abortive search party is organised and when they return in the early morning they notice a motionless figure near the graveyard.

It was Marty, as they had supposed. That evening had been the particular one of the week upon which Grace and herself had been accustomed to privately deposit flowers on Giles's grave, and this was the first occasion since his death eight months earlier on which Grace had failed to keep her appointment. Marty had waited in the road just outside Melbury's, where her fellow-pilgrim had been wont to join her, till she was weary; and at last, thinking that Grace had missed her, and gone on alone, she followed the way to the church, but saw no Grace in front of her. It got later, and Marty continued her walk till she reached the churchyard gate; but still no Grace. Yet her sense of comradeship would not allow her to go on to the grave alone, and still thinking the delay had been unavoidable she stood there with her little basket of flowers in her clasped hands, and her feet chilled by the damp ground, till more than two hours had passed. She then heard the footsteps of Melbury's men, who presently passed on their return from the search. In the silence of the night Marty could not help hearing fragments of their conversation, from which she acquired a general idea of what had occurred, and that Mrs Fitzpiers was by that time in the arms of another man than Giles.

Immediately they had dropped down the hill she entered the churchyard, going to a secluded corner behind the bushes where rose the unadorned stone that marked the last bed of Giles Winterborne. As this solitary and silent girl stood there in the moonlight, a straight slim figure, clothed in a plaitless gown, the contours of womanhood so undeveloped as to be scarcely perceptible in her, the marks of poverty and toil effaced by the misty hour, she touched sublimity at points, and looked almost like a being who had rejected with indifference the attribute of sex for the loftier quality of abstract humanism. She stooped down and cleared away the withered flowers that Grace and herself had laid there the previous week, and put her fresh ones in their place.

'Now, my own, own love,' she whispered, 'you are mine, and only mine; for she has forgot 'ee at last, although for her you died! But I—whenever I get up I'll think of 'ee, and whenever I lie down I'll think of 'ee again. Whenever I plant the young larches I'll think that none can plant as you planted; and whenever I split a gad, and whenever I turn the cider wring, I'll say none could do it like you. If ever I forget your name let me forget home and heaven! . . . But no, no, my love, I never can forget 'ee; for you was a good man, and did good things!'

THOMAS HARDY

Jig

That winter love spoke and we raised no objection, at
Easter 'twas daisies all light and affectionate,
June sent us crazy for natural selection—not
Four traction-engines could tear us apart.
Autumn then coloured the map of our land,
Oaks shuddered and apples came ripe to the hand,
In the gap of the hills we played happily, happpily,
Even the moon couldn't tell us apart.

Grave winter drew near and said, 'This will not do at all—
If you continue, I fear you will rue it all.'
So at the New Year we vowed to eschew it
Although we both knew it would break our heart.
But spring made hay of our good resolutions—
Lovers, you may be as wise as Confucians,
Yet once love betrays you he plays you and plays you
Like fishes for ever, so take it to heart.

C. DAY LEWIS

Hornpipe

Now the peak of summer's past, the sky is overcast
And the love we swore would last for an age seems deceit:
Paler is the guelder since the day we first beheld her
In blush beside the elder drifting sweet, drifting sweet.

Oh quickly they fade—the sunny esplanade,
Speed-boats, wooden spades, and the dunes where we've lain:
Others will be lying amid the sea-pinks sighing
For love to be undying, and they'll sigh in vain.

It's hurrah for each night we have spent our love so lightly
And never dreamed there might be no more to spend at all.
It's goodbye to every lover who thinks he'll live in clover
All his life, for noon is over soon and night-dews fall.

If I could keep you there with the berries in your hair
And your lacy fingers fair as the may, sweet may,
I'd have no heart to do it, for to stay love is to rue it
And the harder we pursue it, the faster it's away.

C. DAY LEWIS

Billy Boy (Northumberland Sea Shanty)

Where hev ye been aal the day, Billy Boy, Billy Boy?
Where hev ye been aal the day, me Billy Boy?
I've been walkin' aal the day
With me charmin' Nancy Grey,
And me Nancy tickl'd me fancy,
Oh me charmin' Billy Boy.

Is she fit to be yor wife,
    Billy Boy, Billy Boy?
Is she fit to be yor wife, me Billy Boy?
    She's as fit to be me wife
    As the fork is to the knife,
    And me Nancy tickl'd me fancy,
    Oh me charmin' Billy Boy.

Can she cook a bit o'steak,
    Billy Boy, Billy Boy?
Can she cook a bit o' steak, me Billy Boy?
    She can cook a bit o' steak,
    Aye, and myek a girdle cake,
    And me Nancy tickl'd me fancy,
    Oh me charmin' Billy Boy.

Can she myek an Irish stew,
    Billy Boy, Billy Boy?
Can she myek an Irish stew, me Billy Boy?
    She can myek an Irish stew,
    Aye, and 'Singin' Hinnies' too,
    And me Nancy tickl'd me fancy,
    Oh me charmin' Billy Boy.

Can she myek a feather bed,
    Billy Boy, Billy Boy?
Can she myek a feather bed, me Billy Boy?
    She can myek a feather bed
    Fit for any sailor's head,
    And me Nancy tickl'd me fancy,
    Oh me charmin' Billy Boy.

ANON

The Prohibition

    Take heed of loving mee,
At least remember, I forbade it thee;
Not that I shall repaire my'unthrifty wast.
Of Breath and Blood, upon thy sighes, and teares,
By being to thee then what to me thou wast;
But, so great Joy, our life at once outweares,
Then, lest thy love, by my death, frustrate bee,
If thou love mee, take heed of loving mee.

    Take heed of hating mee,
Or too much triumph in the Victorie.
Not that I shall be mine owne officer,
And hate with hate againe retaliate;
But thou wilt lose the stile of conquerour,
If I, thy conquest, perish by thy hate.
Then, lest my being nothing lessen thee,
If thou hate mee, take heed of hating mee.

Yet, love and hate mee too,
So, these extreames shall neithers office doe;
Love mee, that I may die the gentler way;
Hate mee, because thy love is too great for mee;
Or let these two, themselves, not me decay;
So shall I, live, thy Stage, not triumph bee;
Lest thou thy love and hate and mee undoe,
To let mee live, O love and hate mee too.

JOHN DONNE

The Ballad of the Sad Café

A humpbacked stranger, Lymon Willis, turns up at Miss Amelia's general shop in a small township. He claims kinship with her and, to everyone's surprise, she offers him a whisky and takes him in. Hitherto she has never invited anyone to her house above the shop. He stays permanently and Miss Amelia begins to serve drinks to her customers—the beginning of the café. He has been there for four years.

Now some explanation is due for all this behaviour. The time has come to speak about love. For Miss Amelia loved Cousin Lymon. So much was clear to everyone. They lived in the same house together and were never seen apart. Therefore, according to Mrs MacPhail, a warty-nosed old busybody who is continually moving her sticks of furniture from one part of the front room to another; according to her and to certain others, these two were living in sin. If they were related, they were only a cross between first and second cousins, and even that could in no way be proved. Now, of course Miss Amelia was a powerful blunderbuss of a person, more than six feet tall—and Cousin Lymon a weakly little hunchback reaching only to her waist. But so much the better for Mrs Stumpy MacPhail and her cronies, for they and their kind glory in conjunctions which are ill-matched and pitiful. So let them be. The good people thought that if those two had found some satisfaction of the flesh between themselves, then it was a matter concerning them and God alone. All sensible people agreed in their opinion about this conjecture—and their answer was a plain, flat *no*. What sort of thing, then, was this love?

First of all, love is a joint experience between two persons—but the fact that it is a joint experience does not mean that it is a similar experience to the two people involved. There are the lover and the beloved, but these two come from different countries. Often the beloved is only a stimulus for all the stored-up love which has lain quiet within the lover for a long time hitherto. And somehow every lover knows this. He feels in his soul that his love is a solitary thing. He comes to know a new, strange loneliness and it is this knowledge which makes him suffer. So there is only one thing for the lover to do. He must house his love within himself as best he can; he must create for himself a whole new inward world—a world intense and strange, complete in himself. Let it be added here that this lover about whom we speak need not necessarily be a young man saving for a wedding ring—this lover can be man, woman, child, or indeed any human creature on this earth.

Now, the beloved can also be of any description. The most outlandish people can be the stimulus for love. A man may be a doddering great-grandfather and still love only a strange girl he saw in the streets of Cheehaw one afternoon two decades past. The preacher may love a fallen woman. The beloved may be treacherous, greasy-headed, and given to evil habits. Yes, and the lover may see this as clearly as anyone else—but that does not affect the evolution of his love one whit. A most mediocre person can be the object of a love which is wild, extravagant, and beautiful as the poison lilies of the swamp. A good man may be the stimulus for a love both violent and debased, or a jabbering madman may bring about in the soul of someone a tender and simple idyll. Therefore, the value of quality of any love is determined solely by the lover himself.

It is for this reason that most of us would rather love than be loved. Almost everyone wants to be the lover. And the curt truth is that, in a deep secret way, the state of being beloved is intolerable to many. The beloved fears and hates the lover, and with the best of reasons. For the lover is for ever trying to strip bare his beloved. The lover craves any possible relation with the beloved, even if this experience can cause him only pain.

CARSON McCULLERS

Romeo and Juliet (Act II Sc ii)

Romeo and Juliet have met for the first time at a dance in her father's house. Their families are at daggers drawn.

ROMEO: He jests at scars that never felt a wound.—

                [Juliet appears above, at a window]

        But, soft! what light through yonder window
          breaks?
        It is the east, and Juliet is the sun!—
        Arise, fair sun, and kill the envious moon,
        Who is already sick and pale with grief,
        That thou her maid art far more fair than she.
        Be not her maid, since she is envious;
        Her vestal livery is but sick and green,
        And none but fools do wear it; cast it off.—
        It is my lady: O, it is my love!
        O, that she knew she were!—
        She speaks, yet she says nothing; what of that?
        Her eye discourses, I will answer it.—
        I am too bold, 'tis not to me she speaks:
        Two of the fairest stars in all the heaven,
        Having some business, do intreat her eyes
        To twinkle in their spheres till they return.
        What if her eyes were there, they in her head?
        The brightness of her cheek would shame those stars,
        As daylight doth a lamp; her eyes in heaven
        Would through the airy region stream so bright,
        That birds would sing and think it were not night.—
        See, how she leans her cheek upon her hand!
        O, that I were a glove upon that hand,
        That I might touch that cheek!

JULIET: Ay me!

ROMEO: She speaks:—

        O, speak again, bright angel! for thou art
        As glorious to this night, being o'er my head,
        As is a winged messenger of heaven
        Unto the white-upturned wondering eyes

Of mortals, that fall back to gaze on him,
When he bestrides the lazy-pacing clouds,
And sails upon the bosom of the air.

JULIET: O Romeo, Romeo! wherefore art thou Romeo?
Deny thy father and refuse thy name;
Or, if thou wilt not, be but sworn my love,
And I'll no longer be a Capulet.

ROMEO: [*Aside*] Shall I hear more, or shall I speak at this?

JULIET: 'Tis but thy name that is my enemy;
Thou art thyself, though not a Montague.
What's Montague? it is nor hand, nor foot,
Nor arm, nor face, nor any other part
Belonging to a man. O, be some other name!—
What's in a name? that which we call a rose,
By any other word would smell as sweet;
So Romeo would, were he not Romeo called,
Retain that dear perfection which he owes,
Without that title.—Romeo, doff thy name,
And for thy name, which is no part of thee,
Take all myself.

ROMEO: I take thee at thy word:
Call me but love, and I'll be new baptized;
Henceforth I never will be Romeo.

JULIET: What man art thou, that thus bescreened in night,
So stumblest on my counsel?

ROMEO: By a name
I know not how to tell thee who I am.
My name, dear saint, is hateful to myself,
Because it is an enemy to thee;
Had I it written, I would tear the word.

JULIET: My ears have yet not drunk a hundred words
Of thy tongue's uttering, yet I know the sound,—
Art thou not Romeo, and a Montague?

ROMEO: Neither, fair maid, if either thee dislike.

JULIET: How cam'st thou hither, tell me, and wherefore?
The orchard walls are high and hard to climb;
And the place death, considering who thou art,
If any of my kinsmen find thee here.

ROMEO: With love's light wings did I o'er-perch these walls;
For stony limits cannot hold love out:
And what love can do, that dares love attempt;
Therefore thy kinsmen are no stop to me.

JULIET: If they do see thee, they will murder thee.

ROMEO: Alack! there lies more peril in thine eye,
Than twenty of their swords; look thou but sweet,
And I am proof against their enmity.

JULIET: I would not for the world they saw thee here.

ROMEO: I have night's cloak to hide me from their eyes;
And, but thou love me, let them find me here:
My life were better ended by their hate,
Than death prorogued, wanting of thy love.

JULIET: By whose direction found'st thou out this place?

ROMEO: By love, that first did prompt me to inquire;
He lent me counsel, and I lent him eyes.
I am no pilot; yet, wert thou as far
As that vast shore washed with the farthest sea,
I should adventure for such merchandise.

JULIET: Thou know'st the mask of night is on my face,
Else would a maiden blush bepaint my cheek
For that which thou hast heard me speak to-night.
Fain would I dwell on form, fain, fain deny
What I have spoke; but farewell compliment!
Dost thou love me? I know thou wilt say 'Ay';
And I will take thy word: yet, if thou swear'st,
Thou mayst prove false; at lovers' perjuries,
They say, Jove laughs. O, gentle Romeo,
If thou dost love, pronounce it faithfully:
Or, if thou think'st I am too quickly won,
I'll frown, and be perverse, and say thee nay,
So thou wilt woo; but else, not for the world.
In truth, fair Montague, I am too fond;
And therefore thou mayst think my 'haviour light.
But trust me, gentleman, I'll prove more true
Than those that have more cunning to be strange.
I should have been more strange, I must confess,
But that thou overheard'st, ere I was ware,

76

My true love passion: therefore pardon me,
And not impute this yielding to light love,
Which the dark night hath so discovered.

ROMEO: Lady, by yonder blessed moon I swear,
That tips with silver all these fruit-tree tops,—

JULIET: O, swear not by the moon, the inconstant moon
That monthly changes in her circled orb,
Lest that thy love prove likewise variable.

ROMEO: What shall I swear by?

JULIET: Do not swear at all;
Or, if thou wilt, swear by thy gracious self,
Which is the god of my idolatry,
And I'll believe thee.

ROMEO: If my heart's dear love—

JULIET: Well, do not swear. Although I joy in thee,
I have no joy of this contract to-night:
It is too rash, too unadvised, too sudden;
Too like the lightning, which doth cease to be,
Ere one can say 'It lightens.' Sweet, good night!
This bud of love, by summer's ripening breath,
May prove a beauteous flower when next we meet
Good night, good night! as sweet repose and rest
Come to thy heart as that within my breast!

ROMEO: O, wilt thou leave me so unsatisfied?

JULIET: What satisfaction canst thou have to-night?

ROMEO: The exchange of thy love's faithful vow for mine.

JULIET: I gave thee mine before thou did'st request it:
And yet I would it were to give again.

ROMEO: Would'st thou withdraw it? for what purpose,
love?

JULIET: But to be frank, and give it thee again.
And yet I wish but for the thing I have:
My bounty is as boundless as the sea,
My love as deep; the more I give to thee,
The more I have, for both are infinite.

                                 [*Nurse calls within*]
I hear some noise within; dear love, adieu!
Anon, good nurse!—Sweet Montague, be true.

Stay but a little, I will come again.   [*Exit*]
ROMEO: O blessed, blessed night! I am afeard,
Being in night, all this is but a dream,
Too flattering-sweet to be substantial.

Re-enter JULIET *above.*

JULIET: Three words, dear Romeo, and good night, indeed.
If that thy bent of love be honourable,
Thy purpose marriage, send me word to-morrow,
By one that I'll procure to come to thee,
Where and what time thou wilt perform the rite;
And all my fortunes at thy foot I'll lay,
And follow thee my lord throughout the world.
NURSE: [*Within*]   Madam!
JULIET: I come, anon.—But if thou mean'st not well,
I do beseech thee—
NURSE: [*Within*] Madam!
JULIET: By and by, I come:—
To cease thy strife and leave me to my grief:
To-morrow will I send.
ROMEO: So thrive my soul,—
JULIET: A thousand times good night!   [*Exit*]
ROMEO: A thousand times the worse to want thy light.
Love goes toward love, as schoolboys from their
    books,
But love from love, toward school with heavy
    looks.
                                        [*Retiring slowly*]

Re-enter JULIET, *above.*

JULIET: Hist! Romeo, hist!—O, for a falconer's voice,
To lure this tassel-gentle back again!
Bondage is hoarse, and may not speak aloud;
Else would I tear the cave where Echo lies,
And make her airy tongue more hoarse than mine
With repetition of my Romeo's name.
ROMEO: It is my soul, that calls upon my name:
How silver-sweet sound lovers' tongues by night,
Like softest music to attending ears!
JULIET: Romeo!

ROMEO: My dear?

JULIET: What o'clock to-morrow
    Shall I send to thee?

ROMEO: By the hour of nine.

JULIET: I will not fail; 'tis twenty years till then.
    I have forgot why I did call thee back.

ROMEO: Let me stand here till thou remember it.

JULIET: I shall forget, to have thee still stand there,
    Rememb'ring how I love thy company.

ROMEO: And I'll still stay, to have thee still forget,
    Forgetting any other home but this.

JULIET: 'Tis almost morning; I would have thee gone,
    And yet no farther than a wanton's bird;
    That lets it hop a little from his hand,
    Like a poor prisoner in his twisted gyves,
    And with a silken thread plucks it back again,
    So loving-jealous of his liberty.

ROMEO: I would I were thy bird.

JULIET: Sweet, so would I;
    Yet I should kill thee with much cherishing.
    Good night, good night! parting is such sweet
        sorrow,
    That I shall say good night till it be morrow. [*Exit*]

ROMEO: Sleep dwell upon thine eyes, peace in thy breast!—
    Would I were sleep and peace, so sweet to rest!
    Hence will I to my ghostly father's close cell;
    His help to crave and my dear hap to tell.   [*Exit*]

WILLIAM SHAKESPEARE

Love Improves The Lover
(from The Anatomy of Melancholy)

Yet for all this, amongst so many irksome, absurd, troublesome symptoms, inconveniences, phantastical fits and passions which are usually incident to such persons, there be some good and graceful qualities in lovers, which this affection causeth. 'As it makes wise men fools, so many times it makes fools become wise; it makes base fellows become generous, cowards courageous,' as Cardan notes out of Plutarch; covetous, liberal and magnificent; clowns, civil; cruel, gentle; wicked profane persons to become religious; slovens, neat; churls, merciful; and dumb dogs, eloquent; your lazy drones, quick and nimble.' *Feras mentes domat cupido*, that fierce, cruel, and rude Cyclops Polyphemus sighed, and shed many a salt tear for Galatea's sake. No passion causeth greater alterations, or more vehement of joy or discontent. Plutarch, *Sympos. lib. 5. quaest.* 1, saith, 'that the soul of a man in love is full of perfumes and sweet odours, and all manner of pleasing tones and tunes, insomuch that it is hard to say (as he adds) whether love do mortal men more harm than good.' It adds spirits and makes them, otherwise soft and silly, generous and courageous, *Audacem faciebat amor*. Ariadne's love made Theseus so adventurous, and Medea's beauty Jason so victorious; *expectorat amor timorem*. Plato is of opinion that the love of Venus made Mars so valorous. 'A young man will be much abashed to commit any foul offence that shall come to the hearing or sight of his mistress.' As he that desired of his enemy now dying, to lay him with his face upward, *ne amasius videret cum a tergo vulneratum*, lest his sweetheart should say he was a coward. 'And if it were possible to have an army consist of lovers, such as love, or are beloved, they would be extraordinary valiant and wise in their government, modesty would detain them from doing amiss, emulation incite them to do that which is good and honest, and a few of them would overcome a great company of others.'

ROBERT BURTON

Two in the Campagna

I wonder do you feel to-day
   As I have felt since, hand in hand,
We sat down on the grass, to stray
   In spirit better through the land,
This morn of Rome and May?

For me, I touched a thought, I know,
   Has tantalized me many times,
(Like turns of thread the spiders throw
   Mocking across our path) for rhymes
To catch at and let go.

Help me to hold it: first it left
   The yellowing fennel, run to seed
There, branching from the brickwork's cleft,
   Some old tomb's ruin: yonder weed
Took up the floating weft,

Where one small orange cup amassed
   Five beetles,—blind and green they grope
Among the honey-meal,—and last,
   Everywhere on the grassy slope
I traced it. Hold it fast!

The champaign with its endless fleece
   Of feathery grasses everywhere!
Silence and passion, joy and peace,
   An everlasting wash of air—
Rome's ghost since her decease.

Such life here, through such lengths of hours,
   Such miracles performed in play,
Such primal naked forms of flowers,
   Such letting Nature have her way
While Heaven looks from its towers.

How say you? Let us, O my dove,
   Let us be unashamed of soul,
As earth lies bare to heaven above.
   How is it under our control
To love or not to love?

I would that you were all to me,
   You that are just so much, no more—
Nor yours, nor mine,—nor slave nor free!
   Where does the fault lie? what the core
Of the wound, since wound must be?

I would I could adopt your will,
   See with your eyes, and set my heart
Beating by yours, and drink my fill
   At your soul's springs,—your part, my part
In life, for good and ill.

No. I yearn upward—touch you close,
   Then stand away. I kiss your cheek,
Catch your soul's warmth,—I pluck the rose
   And love it more than tongue can speak—
Then the good minute goes.

Already how am I so far
   Out of that minute? Must I go
Still like the thistle-ball, no bar,
   Onward, whenever light winds blow,
Fixed by no friendly star?

Just when I seemed about to learn!
   Where is the thread now? Off again!
The old trick! Only I discern—
   Infinite passion, and the pain
Of finite hearts that yearn.

ROBERT BROWNING

Phineas Redux

Phineas, having survived his first wife's death and a trial for murder from which he has been acquitted, is staying with the Duchess of Omnium; Marie Goeseler, an earlier friend, and love is also there: this is their first private encounter since his arrival.

'Do you think that public life then is altogether a mistake, Mr Finn?'

'For a poor man I think that it is, in this country. A man of fortune may be independent; and because he has the power of independence those who are higher than he will not expect him to be subservient. A man who takes to parliamentary office for a living may live by it, but he will have but a dog's life of it.'

'If I were you, Mr Finn, I certainly would not choose a dog's life.'

He said not a word to her on that occasion about herself, having made up his mind that a certain period of the following day should be chosen for the purpose, and he had hardly yet arranged in his mind what words he would use on that occasion. It seemed to him that there would be so much to be said that he must settle beforehand some order of saying it. It was not as though he had merely to tell her of his love. There had been talk of love between them before, on which occasion he had been compelled to tell her that he could not accept that which she offered to him. It would be impossible, he knew, not to refer to that former conversation. And then he had to tell her that he, now coming to her as a suitor and knowing her to be a very rich woman, was himself all but penniless. He was sure, or almost sure, that she was as well aware of this fact as he was himself; but, nevertheless, it was necessary that he should tell her of it,—and if possible so tell her as to force her to believe him when he assured her that he asked her to be his wife, not because she was rich, but because he loved her. It was impossible that all this should be said as they sat side by side in the drawing-room with a crowd of people almost within hearing, and Madame Goesler had just been called upon to play, which she always did directly she was asked. He was invited to make up a rubber, but he could not bring himself to care for cards at the present moment. So he sat apart and listened to the music.

If all things went right with him to-morrow the music,—or the musician who made it,—would be his own for the rest of his life. Was he justified in expecting that she would give him so much? Of her great regard for him as a friend he had no doubt. She had shown it in various ways, and after a fashion that had made it known to all the world. But so had Lady Laura regarded him when he first told her of his love at Lough Linter. She had been his dearest friend, but she had declined to become his wife; and it had been partly so with Violet Effingham, whose friendship to him had been so sweet as to make him for a while almost think that there was more than friendship. Marie Goesler had certainly once loved him;—but so had he once loved Laura Standish. He had been wretched for a while because Lady Laura had refused him. His feelings now were altogether changed, and why should not the feelings of Madame Goesler have undergone a similar change? There was no doubt of her friendship; but then neither was there any doubt of his for Lady Laura. And in spite of her friendship would not revenge be dear to her,—revenge of that nature which a slighted woman must always desire? He had rejected her, and would it not be fair also that he should be rejected? 'I suppose you'll be in your own room before lunch to-morrow,' he said to her as they separated for the night. It had come to pass from the constancy of her visits to Matching in the old Duke's time, that a certain small morning-room had been devoted to her, and this was still supposed to be her property,—so that she was not driven to herd with the public or to remain in her bedroom during all the hours of the morning. 'Yes,' she said; 'I shall go out immediately after breakfast, but I shall soon be driven in by the heat, and then I shall be there till lunch. The Duchess always comes about half-past twelve, to complain generally of the guests.' She answered him quite at her ease, making arrangement for privacy if he should desire it, but doing so as though she thought that he wanted to talk to her about his trial, or about politics, or the place he had just refused. Surely she would hardly have answered him after such a fashion had she suspected that he intended to ask her to be his wife.

At a little before noon the next morning he knocked at her door, and was told to enter. 'I didn't go out after all,' she said. 'I hadn't courage to face the sun.'

'I saw that you were not in the garden.'

'If I could have found you I would have told you that I should be here all the morning. I might have sent you a message, only——only I didn't.'

'I have come——'

'I know why you have come.'

'I doubt that. I have come to tell you that I love you.'

'Oh Phineas;—at last, at last!' And in a moment she was in his arms.

It seemed to him that from that moment all that explanations, and all the statements, and most of the assurances were made by her and not by him. After this first embrace he found himself seated beside her, holding her hand. 'I do not know that I am right,' said he.

'Why not right?'

'Because you are rich and I have nothing.'

'If you ever remind me of that again I will strike you,' she said, raising up her little fist and bringing it down with gentle pressure on his shoulder. 'Between you and me there must be nothing more about that. It must be an even partnership. There must be ever so much about money, and you'll have to go into dreadful details, and make journeys to Vienna to see that the houses don't tumble down;—but there must be no question between you and me of whence it came.'

'You will not think that I have to come to you for that?'

'Have you ever known me to have a low opinion of myself? Is it probable that I shall account myself to be personally so mean and of so little value as to imagine that you cannot love me? I know you love me. But Phineas, I have not been sure till very lately that you would ever tell me so. As for me——! Oh, heavens! when I think of it.'

'Tell me that you love me now.'

'I think I have said so plainly enough. I have never ceased to love you since I first knew you well enough for love. And I'll tell you more,—though perhaps I shall say what you will think condemns me;—you are the only man I ever loved. My husband was very good to me,—and I was, I think, good to him. But he was many years my senior, and I cannot say I loved him,—as I do you.' Then she turned to him, and put her head on his shoulder. 'And I loved the old Duke, too, after a fashion. But it was a different thing from this. I will tell you something about him some day that I have never yet told to a human being.'

'Tell me now.'

'No; not till I am your wife. You must trust me. But I will tell you,' she said, 'lest you should be miserable. He asked me to be his wife.'

'The old Duke?'

'Yes, indeed, and I refused to be a—duchess. Lady Glencora knew it all, and, just at the time, I was breaking my heart,—like a fool, for you! Yes, for you! But I got over it, and am not broken-hearted a bit. Oh, Phineas, I am so happy now.'

Exactly at the time she had mentioned on the previous evening, at half-past twelve, the door was opened, and the Duchess entered the room. 'Oh dear,' she exclaimed, 'perhaps I am in the way; perhaps I am interrupting secrets.'

'No, Duchess.'

'Shall I retire? I will at once if there be anything confidential going on.'

'It has gone on already, and been completed,' said Madame Goesler rising from her seat. 'It is only a trifle. Mr Finn has asked me to be his wife.'

'Well?'

'I couldn't refuse Mr Finn a little thing like that.'

'I should think not, after going all the way to Prague to find a latch-key! I congratulate you, Mr Finn, with all my heart.'

'Thanks, Duchess.'

ANTHONY TROLLOPE

To His Coy Mistress

Had we but world enough and time,
This coyness, lady, were no crime.
We would sit down and think which way
To walk, and pass our long love's day.
Thou by the Indian Ganges' side
Shouldst rubies find; I by the tide
Of Humber should complain. I would
Love you ten years before the flood;
And you should, if you please, refuse
Till the conversion of the Jews.

My vegetable love should grow
Vaster than empires and more slow.
An hundred years should go to praise
Thine eyes, and on thy forehead gaze;
Two hundred to adore each breast;
But thirty thousand for the rest.
An age at least to every part,
And the last age should show your heart.
For, lady, you deserve this state,
Nor would I love at lower rate.
But at my back I always hear
Time's winged chariot hurrying near;
And yonder all before us lie
Deserts of vast eternity.
Thy beauty shall no more be found;
Nor, in thy marble vault, resound
My echoing song; there worms shall try
That long preserved virginity;
And your quaint honour turn to dust,
And into ashes all my lust.
The grave's a fine and private place,
But none, I think, do there embrace.
Now therefore while the youthful hue
Sits on thy skin like morning dew,
And while thy willing soul transpires
At every pore with instant fires,
Now let us sport us while we may,
And now, like amorous birds of prey,
Rather at once our time devour
Than languish in his slow-chapped power.
Let us roll all our strength and all
Our sweetness up into one ball,
And tear our pleasures with rough strife
Thorough the iron gates of life.
Thus, though we cannot make our sun
Stand still, yet we will make him run.

ANDREW MARVELL

The Importance of Being Ernest (Act I)

LADY BRACKNELL *and* ALGERNON *go into the music-room*, GWENDOLEN *remains behind*.

JACK: Charming day it has been, Miss Fairfax.

GWENDOLEN: Pray don't talk to me about the weather, Mr. Worthing. Whenever people talk to me about the weather, I always feel quite certain that they mean something else. And that makes me so nervous.

JACK: I do mean something else.

GWENDOLEN: I thought so. In fact, I am never wrong.

JACK: And I would like to be allowed to take advantage of Lady Bracknell's temporary absence . . .

GWENDOLEN: I would certainly advise you to do so. Mamma has a way of coming back suddenly into a room that I have often had to speak to her about.

JACK (*nervously*): Miss Fairfax, ever since I met you I have admired you more than any girl . . . I have ever met since . . . I met you.

GWENDOLEN: Yes, I am quite well aware of the fact. And I often wish that in public, at any rate, you had been more demonstrative. For me you have always had an irresistible fascination. Even before I met you I was far from indifferent to you. (JACK *looks at her in amazement*.) We live, as I hope you know, Mr Worthing, in an age of ideals. The fact is constantly mentioned in the more expensive monthly magazines, and has now reached the provincial pulpits, I am told; and my ideal has always been to love some one of the name of Ernest. There is something in that name that inspires absolute confidence. The moment Algernon first mentioned to me that he had a friend called Ernest, I knew I was destined to love you.

JACK: You really love me, Gwendolen?

GWENDOLEN: Passionately!

JACK: Darling! You don't know how happy you've made me.

GWENDOLEN: My own Ernest!

JACK: But you don't really mean to say that you couldn't love me if my name wasn't Ernest?

GWENDOLEN: But your name is Ernest.

JACK: Yes, I know it is. But supposing it was something else? Do you mean to say you couldn't love me then?

GWENDOLEN (*glibly*): Ah! that is clearly a metaphysical speculation, and like most metaphysical speculations has very little reference at all to the actual facts of real life, as we know them.

JACK: Personally, darling, to speak quite candidly, I don't much care about the name of Ernest. . . . I don't think the name suits me at all.

GWENDOLEN: It suits you prefectly. It is a divine name. It has a music of its own. It produces vibrations.

JACK: Well, really, Gwendolen, I must say that I think there are lots of other much nicer names. I think Jack, for instance, a charming name.

GWENDOLEN: Jack? . . . No, there is very little music in the name Jack, if any at all, indeed. It does not thrill. It produces absolutely no vibrations. . . . I have known several Jacks, and they all, without exception, were more than usually plain. Besides, Jack is a notorious domesticity for John! And I pity any woman who is married to a man called John. She would probably never be allowed to know the entrancing pleasure of a single moment's solitude. The only really safe name is Ernest.

JACK: Gwendolen, I must get christened at once—I mean we must get married at once. There is no time to be lost.

GWENDOLEN: Married, Mr Worthing?

JACK (*astounded*): Well . . . surely. You know that I love you, and you led me to believe, Miss Fairfax, that you were not absolutely indifferent to me.

GWENDOLEN: I adore you. But you haven't proposed to me yet. Nothing has been said at all about marriage. The subject has not even been touched on.

JACK: Well . . . may I propose to you now?

GWENDOLEN: I think it would be an admirable opportunity. And to spare you any possible disappointment, Mr Worthing, I think it only fair to tell you quite frankly beforehand that I am fully determined to accept you.

JACK: Gwendolen!

GWENDOLEN: Yes, Mr Worthing, what have you got to say to me?

JACK: You know what I have got to say to you.

GWENDOLEN: Yes, but you don't say it.

JACK: Gwendolen, will you marry me? (*Goes on his knees.*)

GWENDOLEN: Of course I will, darling. How long you have

been about it! I am afraid you have had very little experience in how to propose.

JACK: My own one, I have never loved any one in the world but you.

GWENDOLEN: Yes, but men often propose for practice. I know my brother Gerald does. All my girl-friends tell me so. What wonderfully blue eyes you have, Ernest! They are quite, quite blue. I hope you will always look at me just like that, especially when there are other people present.

OSCAR WILDE

To Althea from Prison

When Love with unconfined wings
    Hovers within my Gates;
And my divine *Althea* brings
    To whisper at the Grates:
When I lye tangled in her haire,
    And fetter'd to her eye;
The *Birds*, that wanton in the Aire,
    Know no such Liberty.

When flowing Cups run swiftly round
    With no allaying *Thames*,
Our carelesse heads with Roses bound,
    Our hearts with Loyall Flames;
When thirsty griefe in Wine we steepe,
    When Healths and draughts go free,
Fishes that tipple in the Deepe,
    Know no such Libertie.

When (like committed Linnets) I
  With shriller throat shall sing
The sweetness, Mercy, Majesty,
  And glories of my KING;
When I shall voyce aloud, how Good
  He is, how Great should be;
Inlarged Winds that curle the Flood,
  Know no such Liberty.

Stone Walls doe not a Prison make,
  Nor Iron bars a Cage;
Mindes innocent and quiet take
  That for an Hermitage;
If I have freedome in my Love,
  And in my soule am free;
Angels alone that soar above,
  Injoy such Liberty.

RICHARD LOVELACE

Birds: MS. later altered to *Gods.*

Persuasion

Anne Elliot, who was persuaded by her intolerable family and an interfering friend to refuse Captain Wentworth eight and a half years previously, has, nonetheless, never stopped loving him. Here is her second chance.

She had only time, however, to move closer to the table where he had been writing, when footsteps were heard returning; the door opened, it was himself. He begged their pardon, but he had forgotten his gloves, was again out of the room, almost before Mrs Musgrove was aware of his being in it—the work of an instant!

The revolution which one instant had made in Anne was almost beyond expression. The letter, with a direction hardly legible, to

'Miss A. E——,' was evidently the one which he had been folding so hastily. While supposed to be writing only to Captain Benwick, he had been also addressing her! On the contents of that letter depended all which this world could do for her! Anything was possible, anything might be defied rather than suspense. Mrs Musgrove had little arrangements of her own at her own table; to their protection she must trust, and, sinking into the chair which he had occupied, succeeding to the very spot where he had leaned and written, her eyes devoured the following words:—

'I can listen no longer in silence. I must speak to you by such means as are within my reach. You pierce my soul. I am half agony, half hope. Tell me not that I am too late, that such precious feelings are gone for ever. I offer myself to you again with a heart even more your own than when you almost broke it, eight years and a half ago. Dare not say that man forgets sooner than woman, that his love has an earlier death. I have loved none but you. Unjust I may have been, weak and resentful I have been, but never inconstant. You alone have brought me to Bath. For you alone I think and plan. Have you not seen this? Can you fail to have understood my wishes? I had not waited even these ten days, could I have read your feelings, as I think you must have penetrated mine. I can hardly write. I am every instant hearing something which overpowers me. You sink your voice, but I can distinguish the tones of that voice when they would be lost on others. Too good, too excellent creature! You do us justice, indeed. You do believe that there is true attachment and constancy among men. Believe it to be most fervent, most undeviating, in

'F. W.

'I must go, uncertain of my fate; but I shall return hither, or follow your party, as soon as possible. A word, a look, will be enough to decide whether I enter your father's house this evening, or never.'

Such a letter was not to be soon recovered from. Half an hour's solitude and reflection might have tranquillised her; but the ten minutes only, which now passed before she was interrupted, with all the restraints of her situation, could do nothing towards tranquillity. Every moment rather brought fresh agitation. It was an overpowering happiness. And before she was beyond the first stage of full sensation, Charles, Mary, and Henrietta, all came in.

The absolute necessity of seeming like herself produced then an immediate struggle; but after a while she could do no more. She began not to understand a word they said, and was obliged to plead indisposition and excuse herself. They could then see that she looked very ill—were shocked and concerned—and would not stir without her for the world. This was dreadful. Would they only have gone away, and left her in the quiet possession of that room, it would have been her cure; but to have them all standing or waiting around her was distracting, and, in desperation, she said she would go home.

'By all means, my dear,' cried Mrs Musgrove, 'go home directly, and take care of yourself, that you may be fit for the evening. I wish Sarah was here to doctor you, but I am no doctor myself. Charles, ring and order a chair. She must not walk.'

But the chair would never do. Worse than all! To lose the possibility of speaking two words to Captain Wentworth in the course of her quiet, solitary progress up the town (and she felt almost certain of meeting him) could not be borne. The chair was earnestly protested against; and Mrs Musgrove, who thought only of one sort of illness, having assured herself, with some anxiety, that there had been no fall in the case; that Anne had not, at anytime lately, slipped down, and got a blow on her head; that she was perfectly convinced of having had no fall; could part with her cheerfully, and depend on finding her better at night.

Anxious to omit no possible precaution, Anne struggled, and said—

'I am afraid, ma'am, that it is not perfectly understood. Pray be so good as to mention to the other gentlemen that we hope to see your whole party this evening. I am afraid there has been some mistake; and I wish you particularly to assure Captain Harville and Captain Wentworth that we hope to see them both.'

'Oh, my dear, it is quite understood, I give you my word. Captain Harville has no thought but of going.'

'Do you think so? But I am afraid; and I should be so very sorry. Will you promise me to mention it when you see them again? You will see them both again this morning, I daresay. Do promise me.'

'To be sure I will, if you wish it. Charles, if you see Captain Harville anywhere, remember to give Miss Anne's message. But, indeed, my dear, you need not be uneasy. Captain Harville holds himself quite engaged, I'll answer for it; and Captain Wentworth the same, I daresay.'

Anne could do no more; but her heart prophesied some mischance to damp the perfection of her felicity. It could not be very lasting, however. Even if he did not come to Camden Place himself, it would be in her power to send an intelligible sentence by Captain Harville.

Another momentary vexation occurred. Charles, in his real concern and good nature, would go home with her: there was no preventing him. This was almost cruel. But she could not be long ungrateful; he was sacrificing an engagement at a gunsmith's to be of use to her; and she set off with him, with no feeling but gratitude apparent.

They were in Union Street, when a quicker step behind, a something of familiar sound, gave her two moments' preparation for the sight of Captain Wentworth. He joined them; but, as if irresolute whether to join or to pass on, said nothing—only looked. Anne could command herself enough to receive that look, and not repulsively. The cheeks which had been pale now glowed, and the movements which had hesitated were decided. He walked by her side. Presently, struck by a sudden thought, Charles said—

'Captain Wentworth, which way are you going? only to Gay Street, or farther up the town?'

'I hardly know,' replied Captain Wentworth, surprised.

'Are you going as high as Belmont? Are you going near Camden Place? Because, if you are, I shall have no scruple in asking you to take my place, and give Anne your arm to her father's door. She is rather done for this morning, and must not go so far without help; and I ought to be at that fellows' in the market place. He promised me the sight of a capital gun he is just going to send off; said he would keep it unpacked to the last possible moment, that I might see it; and if I do not turn back now, I have no chance. By his description, it is a good deal like the second-sized double-barrel of mine, which you shot with one day round Winthrop.'

There could not be an objection. There could be only a most proper alacrity, a most obliging compliance for public view; and smiles reined in and spirits dancing in private rapture. In half a minute, Charles was at the bottom of Union Street again, and the other two proceeding together; and soon words enough had passed between them to decide their direction towards the comparatively quiet and retired gravel walk, where the power of conversation would make the present hour a blessing indeed; and prepare it for all the immortality which the happiest recollections of their own future lives could bestow. There they exchanged again those feelings and those promises which had once before seemed to secure everything, but which had been followed by so many, many years of division and estrangement. There they returned again into the past, more exquisitely happy, perhaps, in their re-union, than when it had been first projected; more tender, more tried, more fixed in a knowledge of each other's character, truth, and attachment; more equal to act, more justified in acting. And there, as they slowly paced the gradual ascent, heedless of every group around them, seeing neither sauntering politicians, bustling housekeepers, flirting girls, nor nurserymaids and children, they could indulge in those retrospections and acknow-ledgments, and especially in those explanations of what had directly preceded the present moment, which were so poignant and so ceaseless in interest. All the little variations of the last week were gone through; and of yesterday and to-day there could scarcely be an end.

JANE AUSTEN

Presents

See, see, mine own sweet jewel,
What have I for my darling:
A robin-redbreast and a starling.
These I give both in hope to move thee;
Yet thou say'st I do not love thee.

ANON

Our Hearts

Mariolle's eyes always searched among the letters for the longed-for handwriting. When he had found it, an involuntary emotion would surge up in his heart, making it throb wildly; he always took this letter first, and would dwell on the address before tearing open the envelope. What would she say? Would the word 'love' be there? She had never yet used that word without adding 'well' or 'very much'; 'I love you well' or 'I love you very much'. How thoroughly he was used to this formula that lost all power by using additional words! Can there be much or little in loving?

To love 'very much' is to love poorly: one loves—that is all—it cannot be modified or completed without being nullified. It is a short word, but it contains all: it means the body, the soul, the life, the entire being. We feel it as we feel the warmth of the blood, we breathe it as we breathe the air, we carry it in ourselves as we carry our thoughts. Nothing more exists for us. It is not a word; it is an inexpressible state indicated by four letters. . . .

GUY DE MAUPASSANT

Quoth John to Joan

Quoth John to Joan, will thou have me:
I prithee now, wilt? and I'll marry thee,
My cow, my calf, my house, my rents,
And all my lands and tenements:
   O, say, my Joan, will not that do?
   I cannot come every day to woo.

I've corn and hay in the barn hard-by,
And three fat hogs pent up in the sty,
I have a mare and she is coal black,
I ride on her tail to save my back.
   Then, say, my Joan, will not that do?
   I cannot come every day to woo.

I have a cheese upon the shelf,
And I cannot eat it all myself;
I've three good marks that lie in a rag,
In a nook of the chimney, instead of a bag.
    Then, say, my Joan, will not that do?
    I cannot come every day to woo.

To marry I would have thy consent,
But faith I never could compliment;
I can say nought but 'Hoy, gee ho!'
Words that belong to the cart and the plough.
    Oh, say, my Joan, will not that do?
    I cannot come every day to woo.

ANON

On Women and Wives (from The Talmud)

Love thy wife as thyself; honour her more than thyself. He who lives unmarried, lives without joy. He who sees his wife die has, as it were, been present at the destruction of the sanctuary itself. The children of a man who marries for money will prove a curse to him. All the blessings of a household come through the wife, therefore should her husband honour her.

Rab said:

'Men should be careful lest they cause a woman to weep, for God counts their tears.

'In cases of charity, where both men and women claim relief, the latter should be first assisted. If there should not be enough for both, the men should cheerfully relinquish their claims.

'A woman's death is felt by nobody as by her husband.

'Tears are shed on God's altar for one who forsakes his first love.

'He who loves his wife as himself, and honours her more than himself, will train his children properly; he will meet, too, the fulfillment of the verse, "And thou shalt know that there is peace in thy tent, and thou wilt look over thy habitation and shalt miss nothing" (Job 5:24).'

Rabbi José said:

'I never call my wife "wife", but "home", for she, indeed, makes my home.'

Queen Victoria Proposes to Albert

Next morning, about half past twelve, the Prince was summoned to a private audience. 'I said to him' wrote the Queen 'that I thought he must be aware *why* I wished them to come here, and that it would make me *too happy* if he would consent to what I wished (to marry me); we embraced each other over and over again, and he was *so* kind, *so* affectionate; Oh! to *feel* I was, and am, loved by *such* an Angel as Albert was *too great delight to describe!* he is *perfection;* perfection in every way—in beauty—in everything! I told him I was quite unworthy of him and kissed his dear hand—he said he would be very happy "das Leben mit dir zu zubringen" [to share life with you] and was so kind and seemed so happy, that I really felt it was the happiest brightest moment in my life, which made up for all I had suffered and endured. Oh! *how* I adore and love him, I cannot say!! *how* I will strive to make him feel as little as possible the great sacrifice he has made; I told him it was a great sacrifice,—which he wouldn't allow. . . . I feel the happiest of human beings.'

'He [Prince Albert] was *so* affectionate, *so* kind, *so* dear,' wrote the Queen' 'we kissed each other again and again and he called me [in German] "Darling little one, I love you *so* much" and that we should have a very fortunate life together. Oh! what *too* sweet delightful moments are these!! Oh! how *blessed*, how happy I am to think he is *really* mine; I can scarcely believe myself *so* blessed. I kissed his dear hand and do feel *so* grateful to him; he is such an Angel, such a *very* great Angel! We sit so nicely side by side on that little blue sofa; no two Lovers could ever be happier than we are! . . . He took my hands in his, and said my hands were so little he could hardly believe they *were* hands, as he had hitherto *only* been accustomed to handle hands like Ernest's.'

Here is the first night of the honeymoon.

When the Queen had looked over the rooms she and the Prince were to occupy and changed her dress, she joined the Prince in his room; he was playing the piano and had changed into his Windsor coat. He took the Queen in his arms and kissed and caressed her, and 'was so dear and kind. We had our dinner in our sitting room, but I had such a sick headache that I could eat nothing, and was obliged to lie down . . . for the remainder of the evening on the sofa; but ill or not, I _never, never_ spent such an evening!! My _dearest dearest dear_ Albert sat on a footstool by my side, and his excessive love and affection gave me feelings of heavenly love and happiness I never could have _hoped_ to have felt before! He clasped me in his arms, and we kissed each other again and again! His beauty, his sweetness and gentleness—really how can I ever be thankful enough to have such a _Husband!_ . . . to be called by names of tenderness, I have never yet heard used to me before—was bliss beyond belief! Oh! this was the happiest day of my life!—May God help me to do my duty as I ought and be worthy of such blessings!'

Next day to have the Prince's 'beautiful angelic face' to greet her in the morning was more joy than the Queen could express. They got up at half past eight, much earlier than the Queen's usual hour, and Greville, still grumpy, told Lady Palmerston the wedding night had been too short, this was 'not the way to provide us with a Prince of Wales'. Albert breakfasted in a black velvet jacket without any neckcloth so that his throat could be seen 'and looked more beautiful' wrote the Queen 'than it is possible for me to say'. They then walked on the Terrace and New Walk, alone arm in arm. It was now the turn of the Prince to feel sick, as he had not yet recovered from the effects of his seasickness followed by the festivities and banquets attendant on the marriage in addition to the strain of the ceremony itself. He lay down and dozed in the Queen's sitting-room while she wrote letters, getting up at one point to read her a funny story but feeling so poorly that he was forced to lie down again, resting his head on her shoulder. That evening, the second of the honeymoon, was not spent alone with the Queen. There were ten people at dinner, a 'very delightful merry, nice little party' wrote the Queen. Prince Albert recovered sufficiently to be able to sing, though he still felt weak in his knees.

Lady Mary Wortley Montagu (then Pierrepont) to E. W. Montagu

March 1711.

Though your letter is far from what I expected, having once promised to answer it, with the sincere account of my inmost thoughts, I am resolved you shall not find me worse than my word, which is (whatever you may think) inviolable.

'Tis no affection to say, that I despise the pleasure of pleasing people whom I despise: all the fine equipages that shine in the ring never gave me another thought than either pity or contempt gave me for the owners, that could place happiness in attracting the eyes of strangers. Nothing touches me with satisfaction but what touches my heart, and I should find more pleasure in the secret joy I should feel at a kind expression from a friend I esteemed, than at the admiration of a whole playhouse, or the envy of those of my own sex who could not attain to the same number of jewels, fine clothes, etc., supposing I was at the very summit of this sort of happiness.

You may be this friend if you please. Did you really esteem me, had you any tender regard for me, I could, I think, pass my life in any station, happier with you than in all the grandeur of the world with any other. You have some humours, that would be disagreeable to any woman that married with an intention of finding her happiness abroad. That is not my resolution. If I marry, I propose to myself a retirement; there is few of my acquaintance I should ever wish to see again; and the pleasing one, and only one, is the way in which I design to please myself. Happiness is the natural design of all the world; and everything we see done, is meant in order to attain it. My imagination places it in friendship. By friendship, I mean an entire communication of thoughts, wishes, interests, and pleasures, being undivided; a mutual esteem, which naturally carries with it a pleasing sweetness of conversation, and terminates in the desire of making one or another happy, without being forced to run into visits, noise, and hurry, which serve rather to trouble than compose the thoughts of any reasonable creature. There are few capable of a friendship such as I have described, and 'tis necessary for the generality of the world to be taken up with trifles. Carry a fine lady or a fine gentleman out of town, and they know no more what to say. To take from them plays, operas, and fashions, is taking away all their topics of discourse; and they know not how to form their thoughts on any other subjects. They know very well what it is to be admired, but are perfectly ignorant of what it is to be loved. I take you to have sense enough not to think this science romantic: I rather choose to use the word friendship than love, because in the general sense that word is spoke, it signifies a passion rather founded on fancy than reason; and when I say friendship, I mean a mixture of friendship and esteem, and which a long acquaintance increases, not decays; how far I deserve such a friendship, I can be no judge of myself: I may want the good sense that is necessary to be agreeable to a man of merit, but I know I want the vanity to believe I have; and can promise you shall never like me less, upon knowing me better; and that I shall never forget that you have a better understanding than myself.

And now let me entreat you to think (if possible) tolerably of my modesty, after so bold a declaration: I am resolved to throw off reserve, and use me ill if you please. I am sensible to own an inclination for a man is putting oneself wholly in his power; but sure you have generosity enough not to abuse it. After all I have said, I pretend no tie but on your heart: if you do not love me, I shall not be happy with you; if you do I need add no further. I am not mercenary, and would not receive an obligation that comes not from one who loves me. I do not desire my letter back again: you have honour, and I dare trust you. I am going to the same place I went last spring. I shall think of you there: it depends upon you in what manner.

M.P.

Saint-Simon at Versailles
Here he is writing about his own father and Louis XIII.

The King had fallen deeply in love with Mlle d'Hautefort. He visited the Queen more often on her account, and talked much with her. He also spoke of her constantly to my father, who saw clearly that he was smitten. My father was young and gallant at that time, and he could not understand the King being so much in love, so little able to conceal it, and yet going no further in the matter. He judged that timidity must be the cause, and one day when the King was talking passionately about the lady, he acted on that assumption and offered his services as ambassador, to bring the affair to a successful conclusion. The King let him speak; then, looking very stern, said, 'It is true that I am in love, that I am sensible of the fact, that I enjoy speaking of her, and think of her still more often. It is also true that all this happens in spite of myself, because I am a man and therefore weak in this respect. But since my position as King makes it easy for me to gratify my passion, I must be doubly careful to avoid sin and scandal. I forgive you this time because of your youth, but never let me hear you speak like this again, if you wish me to continue to be your friend.' This speech descended on my father like a thunderbolt, and the scales fell from his eyes. The idea that the King was timid in love vanished in the light of his pure, triumphant virtue. This was the lady whom the King appointed lady-in-waiting to the Queen, and caused to be addressed as Mme d'Hautefort. In the end she became the second wife of the last Maréchal de Schonberg, by whom she had no children. Since that time, spinster ladies-in-waiting have always been given the title of Madame.

My father never recovered from the death of Louis XIII, never spoke of him without tears in his eyes, never referred to him but as 'the King, my master', and never missed going every year on May 14th to his memorial service, at Saint-Denis, or having a solemn mass said for him at Blaye.

The Young Visiters

The hero proposes to the heroine.

She looked very beautifull with some red roses in her hat and the
dainty red ruge in her cheeks looked quite the thing. Bernard
heaved a sigh and his eyes flashed as he beheld her and Ethel
thorght to herself what a fine type of manhood he reprisented . . .

Bernard sat beside her in profound silence gazing at her pink
face and long wavy eye lashes. . . .

Ethel he murmured in a trembly voice.

Oh what is it said Ethel hastily sitting up.

Words fail me ejaculated Bernard horsly my passion for you is
intense he added fervently. It has grown day and night since I first
beheld you.

Oh said Ethel in supprise I am not prepared for this and she
lent back against the trunk of the tree.

Bernard placed one arm tightly round her. When will you marry
me Ethel he uttered you must be my wife it has come to that I love
you so intensly that if you say no I shall perforce dash my body
to the brink of yon muddy river he panted wildly.

Oh dont do that implored Ethel breathing rarther hard.

Then say you love me he cried.

Oh Bernard she sighed fervently I certainly love you madly you
are to me like a Heathen god she cried looking at his manly form
and handsome flashing face I will indeed marry you.

DAISY ASHFORD

Irish Song

I know where I'm going
And I know who's going with me:
I know who I love,
But the dear knows who I'll marry.

I have stockings of silk,
Shoes of fine green leather,
Combs to buckle my hair,
And a ring for every finger.

Some say he's black,
But I say he's bonny,
The fairest of them all,
My handsome winsome Johnny.

Feather beds are soft,
And painted rooms are bonny,
But I would leave them all
To go with my love Johnny.

I know where I'm going,
And I know who's going with me:
I know who I love,
But the dear knows who I'll marry.

ANON

Part III

IDYLLIC LOVE

It is not really surprising that there is less to choose from here; people without earache hardly ever remark upon the absence of pain and when we are idyllically happy we communicate it by what we are, rather than by anything that we say. This may be the chief reason why perfect happiness is not easy to write about: good or happy characters often emerge as smug and tedious (look at Dickens—although his failure in this one respect was probably due to an over-simplified morality with few of the finer, or more interesting, shades). But there is a certain fascination in reflecting upon the number of well known writers who were utterly incapable of writing about love: Shaw comes instantly to mind. There are, of course, a number of novelists who have written marvellously about it (Hardy, in *Jude the Obscure*, Richardson in *Clarissa* are but two examples), but whose work does not contain the encapsulation that is needed for an anthology.

However, what *is* here has all the sharp and aromatic sweetness of honey taken from privileged bees. There is the feeling of nervous excitement in Rosamond Lehmann's piece from *The Weather in the Streets* when Olivia begins her affair with Rollo; the marvellous affection that is only generated by mutually successful sex (*The Duchess of Malfi*, Count Mosca in *The Charterhouse of Parma*); the perfect adventure—amazing events, with a joyful ending in the right company ('The Owl and The Pussy Cat'); the sense of cosmic transformation that can accompany deep love (Tolstoy—Levin again). Last of the prose excerpts there is the miracle of reality that love can sometimes perform—the overwhelming sense of understanding that simply increases everyday love—here presented by Henry Green, one of the half dozen best novelists of this century and, like Elizabeth Taylor, distressingly under-read. Green writes with a poet's eye for essential accuracy: he manages to be funny and touching yet at the same time writing passages of great beauty: this short piece from *Back* is also floodlit with love.

Contents

The Extasie

Where, like a pillow on a bed,
  A Pregnant banke swel'd up, to rest
The violets reclining head,
  Sat we two, one anothers best.
Our hands were firmely cimented
  With a fast balme, which thence did spring,
Our eye-beames twisted, and did thred
  Our eyes, upon one double string;
So to'entergraft our hands, as yet
  Was all the meanes to make us one,
And pictures in our eyes to get
  Was all our propagation.
As 'twixt two equall Armies, Fate
  Suspends uncertaine victorie,
Our soules, (which to advance their state,
  Were gone out,) hung 'twixt her, and mee.
And whil'st our soules negotiate there,
  Wee like sepulchrall statues lay;
All day, the same our postures were,
  And wee said nothing, all the day.
If any, so by love refin'd,
  That he soules language understood,
And by good love were growen all minde,
  Within convenient distance stood,
He (though he knew not which soul spake,
  Because both meant, both spake the same)
Might thence a new concoction take,
  And part farre purer than he came.
This Extasie doth unperplex
  (We said) and tell us what we love,
Wee see by this, it was not sexe,
  Wee see, we saw not what did move:
But as all severall soules containe
  Mixture of things, they know not what,
Love, these mixt soules, doth mixe againe,
  And makes both one, each this and that.

A single violet transplant,
    The strength, the colour, and the size,
(All which before was poore, and scant,)
    Redoubles still, and multiplies.
When love, with one another so
    Interinanimates two soules,
That abler soule, which thence doth flow,
    Defects of lonelinesse controules.
Wee then, who are this new soule, know,
    Of what we are compos'd, and made,
For, th'Atomies of which we grow,
    Are soules, whom no change can invade.
But O alas, so long, so farre
    Our bodies why doe wee forbeare?
They are ours, though they are not wee, Wee are
    The intelligences, they the spheares.
We owe them thankes, because they thus,
    Did us, to us, at first convay,
Yeelded their forces, sense, to us,
    Nor are drosse to us, but allay.
On man heavens influence workes not so,
    But that it first imprints the ayre,
Soe soule into the soule may flow,
    Though it to body first repaire.
As our blood labours to beget
    Spirits, as like soules as it can,
Because such fingers need to knit
    That subtile knot, which makes us man:
So must pure lovers soules descend
    T'affections, and to faculties
Which sense may reach and apprehend,
    Else a great Prince in prison lies.
To'our bodies turne wee then, that so
    Weake men on love reveal'd may looke;
Loves mysteries in soules doe grow,
    But yet the body is his booke.
And if some lover, such as wee,
    Have heard this dialogue of one,

Let him still marke us, he shall see
Small change, when we'are to bodies gone.

JOHN DONNE

The Weather in the Streets

This is the sequel to Invitation To The Waltz. *Olivia who has been married and is separated from her husband encounters Rollo Spencer again at his family's house in the country. Rollo is also married. Here is the first time he calls on her in her flat one evening.*

'Darling, are you glad to see me?' Coaxing. . .
   'Yes, Rollo.'
'Don't be frightened,' he said.
   It was all before now, it could still be nothing, never happen. . . . I don't know how, there wasn't one moment, but he made it all come easy and right as he always did, saying: 'She won't be coming in, will she?'
   'Not before midnight, anyway. . . .'
   His head looked round the room quickly, over my head. 'Not here,' I said. If it had to be it must be where it was me, not Etty. . . . It must be more serious and important. . . . 'Wait. I'll call.'
   Running upstairs, one flight, past Etty's bedroom, another flight, my bedroom, my own things. That was better. Bed, books, dressing-table, arm-chair, my picture of people sitting on park chairs under a plane-tree, sun-dappled—a woman with a pram, another with a red sunshade—my picture I bought with Ivor at the London group, with a wedding cheque, and was so excited, that was still all right to live with, though not so good as I'd thought. I turned up the gas-fire and switched on the bedside lamp with its shade Anna did. I thought: He must think everything nice, not tartish, undressing quickly, and my red silk dressing-gown on, tied tightly, it had to be wonderful, not sordid, thinking: This tremendous step, I must tell him, explain. . . . But it was already the space in between where no deciding is, and no emotion. . . . His loud step came up the stairs, he came in quickly as if he knew

109

the room. 'I couldn't stay down there any longer.' Not looking round, but only at me. That's the thing about him, it always was, from the beginning—his directness—no constraint, awkwardness or head-doubts about what he wants, acting on a kind of smooth, warm impetus, making it all so right and easy. . . . Saying: 'Oh, darling, I knew you'd be beautiful.' Delighted. . . . 'It's rather a step,' I tried to say, but already it wasn't any more.

This part, in fact, precedes the foregoing scene in the book.

It was then the time began when there wasn't any time. The journey was in the dark, going on without end or beginning, without landmarks, bearings lost: asleep? . . . waking? . . . Time whirled, throwing up in paradoxical slow motion a sign, a scene, sharp, startling, lingering as a blow over the heart. A look flared, urgently meaning something, stamping itself for ever, ever, ever. . . . Gone, flashed away, a face in a train passing, not ever to be recovered. A voice called out, saying words—going on, on, on, eternally reverberating . . . fading out, a voice of tin, a hollow voice, the plain meaning lost, the echo meaningless. A voice calling out by night in a foreign station where the night train draws through, not stopping. . . .

There was this inward double living under amorphous impacts of dark and light mixed: that was when we were together. . . . Not being together was a vacuum. It was an unborn place in the shadow of the time before and the time to come. It was remembering and looking forward, drawn out painfully both ways, taut like a bit of elastic. . . . Wearing. . . .

There were no questions in this time. All was agreeing, answer after answer melting, lapsing into one another: 'Yes'; 'Yes, darling'; 'Yes'—smiling, accepting, kissing, dismissing. . . . No argument, no discussion. No separate character any more to judge, test, learn by degrees. He was like breathing, like the heart beating—unknown, essential, mysterious. He was like the dark. . . .

Well, I know what it is to be in love all right. . . .

ROSAMOND LEHMANN

The Song of Solomon

Behold, thou art fair, my love; behold, thou art fair; thou hast doves' eyes within thy locks: thy hair is as a flock of goats, that appear from mount Gilead.

2. Thy teeth are like a flock of sheep that are even shorn, which came up from the washing; whereof every one bear twins, and none is barren among them.

3. Thy lips are like a thread of scarlet, and thy speech is comely: thy temples are like a piece of pomegranate within thy locks.

4. Thy neck is like the tower of David builded for an armoury, whereon there hang a thousand bucklers, all shields of mighty men.

5. Thy breasts are like two young roes that are twins, which feed among the lilies.

6. Until the day break, and the shadows flee away, I will get me to the mountain of myrrh, and to the hill of frankincense.

7. Thou art all fair, my love; there is no spot in thee.

8. Come with me from Lebanon, my spouse, with me from Lebanon: look from the top of Amana, from the top of Shenir and Hermon, from the lions' dens, from the mountains of the leopards.

9. Thou hast ravished my heart, my sister, my spouse; thou hast ravished my heart with one of thine eyes, with one chain of thy neck.

10. How fair is thy love, my sister, my spouse! how much better is thy love than wine! and the smell of thine ointments than all spices!

11. Thy lips, O my spouse, drop as the honeycomb: honey and milk are under thy tongue; and the smell of thy garments is like the smell of Lebanon.

12. A garden inclosed is my sister, my spouse; a spring shut up, a fountain sealed.

13. Thy plants are an orchard of pomegranates, with pleasant fruits; camphire, with spikenard,

14. Spikenard and saffron; calamus and cinnamon, with all trees of frankincense; myrrh and aloes, with all the chief spices:

15. A fountain of gardens, a well of living waters, and streams from Lebanon.

The Good-Morrow

I wonder by my troth, what thou, and I
Did, till we lov'd? were we not wean'd till then?
But suck'd on countrey pleasures, childishly?
Or snorted we in the seaven sleepers den?
T'was so; But this, all pleasures fancies bee.
If ever any beauty I did see,
Which I desir'd, and got, t'was but a dreame of thee.

And now good morrow to our waking soules,
Which watch not one another out of feare;
For love, all love of other sights controules,
And makes one little roome, an every where.
Let sea-discoverers to new worlds have gone,
Let Maps to other, worlds on worlds have showne,
Let us possesse one world, each hath one, and is one.

My face in thine eye, thine in mine appears,
And true plaine hearts doe in the faces rest,
Where can we finde two better hemispheares
Without sharpe North, without declining West?
What ever dyes, was not mixt equally;
If our two loves be one, or, thou and I
Love so alike, that none doe slacken, none can die.

JOHN DONNE

Juliette Drouet to Victor Hugo (1833)

To my beloved,
   I have left you, my beloved. May the memory of my love follow
and comfort you during our separation. If you only knew how
much I love you, how essential you are to my life, you would not
dare to stay away for an instant, you would always remain by my
side, your heart pressed close to my heart, your soul to my soul.

It is now eleven o'clock in the evening. I have not seen you. I am waiting for you with great impatience, as I will wait for you always. It seems a whole century since I last saw you, since I last looked upon your features and became intoxicated with your gaze. Given my ill-luck, I shall probably not see you tonight.

Oh! come back, my love, my life, come back.

If you knew how I long for you, how the memory of last night leaves me delirious with joy and full of desire. How I long to give myself up in ecstasy to your sweet breath and to those kisses from your lips which fill me with delight!

My Victor, forgive me all my extravagances. They are a further token of my love. Love me. I need your love as a touchstone of my existence. It is the sun which breathes life into me.

I am going to bed. I shall fall asleep praying of you. My need to see you happy gives me faith.

My last waking thoughts, and all my dreams, are of you.

Juliette

The Duchess of Malfi

A married lovers' talk—one of the few sunlit moments in this sombre work. The Duchess and Antonio are secretly married. Cariola is the Duchess's waiting-woman.

DUCHESS: Bring me the casket hither, and the glass.—
You get no lodging here to-night, my lord.
ANTONIO: Indeed, I must persuade one.
DUCHESS: Very good:
I hope in time 'twill grow into a custom,
That noblemen shall come with cap and knee
To purchase a night's lodging of their wives.
ANTONIO: I must lie here.
DUCHESS: Must! you are a lord of misrule.
ANTONIO: Indeed, my rule is only in the night.
DUCHESS: To what use will you put me?
ANTONIO: We'll sleep together.
DUCHESS: Alas,
What pleasure can two lovers find in sleep!

CARIOLA: My lord, I lie with her often; and I know
She'll much disquiet you.
ANTONIO: See, you are complained of.
CARIOLA: For she's the sprawling'st bedfellow.
ANTONIO: I shall like her
The better for that.
CARIOLA: Sir, shall I ask you a question?
ANTONIO: Oh, I pray thee, Cariola:
CARIOLA: Wherefore still, when you lie
With my lady, do you rise so early?
ANTONIO: Labouring men
Count the clock oftenest, Cariola, are glad
When their task's ended.
DUCHESS: I'll stop your mouth.
                       [*Kisses him*]
ANTONIO: Nay, that's but one; Venus had two soft doves
To draw her chariot; I must have another.
                     [*She kisses him again*]
When wilt thou marry, Cariola?
CARIOLA: Never, my lord.
ANTONIO: Oh, fie upon this single life! forgo it.
We read how Daphne, for her peevish flight,
Became a fruitless bay-tree; Syrinx turned
To the pale empty reed; Anaxarete
Was frozen into marble: whereas those
Which married, or proved kind unto their friends,
Were by a gracious influence transhaped
Into the olive, pomegranate, mulberry,
Became flowers, precious stones, or eminent stars.
CARIOLA: This is a vain poetry: but I pray you tell me,
If there were proposed me, wisdom, riches, and
    beauty,
In three several young men, which should I
    choose?
ANTONIO: 'Tis a hard question: this was Paris' case,
And he was blind in 't, and there was great
    cause;
For how was't possible he could judge right,

Having three amorous goddesses in view,
And they stark naked? 'twas a motion
Were able to benight the apprehension
Of the severest counsellor of Europe.
Now I look on both your faces so well form'd,
It puts me in mind of a question I would ask.

CARIOLA: What is 't?

ANTONIO: I do wonder why hard-favour'd ladies,
For the most part, keep worse-favour'd
    waiting-women
To attend them, and cannot endure fair ones.

DUCHESS: Oh, that's soon answer'd.
Did you ever in your life know an ill painter
Desire to have his dwelling next door to the shop
Of an excellent picture-maker? 'twould disgrace
His face-making, and undo him. I prithee,
When were we so merry?—My hair tangles.

ANTONIO: Pray thee, Cariola, let's steal forth the room,
And let her talk to herself; I have divers times
Served her the like, when she hath chafed
    extremely.
I love to see her angry. Softly, Cariola.

[Exeunt Antonio and Cariola]

JOHN WEBSTER

Napoleon Bonaparte to Josephine Beauharnais

Paris, December 1795

I wake filled with thoughts of you. Your portrait and the intoxicating evening which we spent yesterday have left my senses in turmoil. Sweet, incomparable Josephine, what a strange effect you have on my heart! Are you angry? Do I see you looking sad? Are you worried? . . . My soul aches with sorrow, and there can be no rest for your lover; but is there still more in store for me when, yielding to the profound feelings which overwhelm me, I draw from your lips, from your heart a love which consumes me with fire? Ah! it was last night that I fully realised how false an image of you your portrait gives!

You are leaving at noon; I shall see you in three hours.

Until then, mio dolce amor, a thousand kisses; but give me none in return, for they set my blood on fire.

Sonnet
(From Moods of Love)

See, at a turn of her wrist, paradise open;
Dote, lover, upon a turquoise vein;
Feel how the blood flowers and the nerves go lilting
Like butterflies through an immortal blue.
This is creation morning. What could happen
But miracles here? The god you entertain,
The pure legend you breathe, no desert silting
Over your garden ever makes untrue.

New-seen, first-named, your own to hurt and heal,
This commonplace of skin, bone, habit, sense
Is now a place that never was before.
Lose and possess yourself therein: adore
The ideal clay, the carnal innocence.
Where all's miraculous, all is most real.

C. DAY LEWIS

Call It Love

This is a barely fictionalised account of the author's meetings with her husband Maxim Litvinov who was allowed to return to Russia in exchange for R. H. Bruce Lockhart who had been imprisoned in Moscow for alleged espionage.

Mr Belking held a typewritten letter up to his glasses and cleared his throat, but instead of beginning to dictate he said, not looking up from the letter, 'I have something to ask you.'

Eileen blushed thickly.

'Will you give me perhaps English lessons?'

He looked up sharply and Eileen was sure he had observed her crimson cheeks. 'I've never given a lesson in my life,' she faltered.

Mr Belkin leaned back in his chair, even crossed his knees. 'If you could explain me the use of the present perfect?'

'Which would that be?'

Mr Belkin sighed. 'We could read,' he said, and sighed again, and asked permission to smoke.

After taking out a cigarette, he laid the pack on the table, and Eileen shook a couple onto the letter file. 'There's hardly any tobacco in them!' she said.

'Russian cigarettes. Together with mouthpiece. Very hygienical.'

'Can you get them in London?'

'I bring them with. They wished to take them away at Dover— too many, they told—but I say, "I thought England would let me to smoke cigarettes of my native land." And custom man smile and put crosses on every box. I hear him say to man next him, "Chap homesick".'

Eileen took the lid off her typewriter, but at that very moment a high clear voice was heard from the bottom of the stairs, asking the landlady if Miss Shelly was in. Eileen darted to the door and turned the key in the lock. The unseen caller mounted the stairs and knocked again and again, trying the handle between knocks, before giving up and clattering slowly down the stairs. Even after they heard the click of heels on the flags outside, the two in the room only ventured to speak in undertones. It was beginning to get dark in the room, and Eileen lit the gas before sitting down to nudge a sheet of paper into the typewriter. She typed Mr Belkin's address and the date at the top right-hand corner of the paper and swung the carriage back to write 'Dear Sirs' lower down. But there was to be no more typing that day. She got up and perched on the arm of Mr Belkin's chair. Immediately his arm came round her waist and drew her against his hard, firm thigh. She felt urgent kisses in the very middle of her cheek, but when she turned to receive them on her lips Mr Belkin moved his away. 'Not hygienical,' he said. Eileen pulled herself back and sat bolt upright on the arm of the chair. He passed a plump, white hand over his flushed face and smoothed the hair off his forehead. 'In my country,' he said, 'girls do not kiss unless they are ready for all.'

Eileen could not honestly tell herself that she was ready for All at the moment—a few more preliminaries, she thought, would have been in order—but she could not refuse something that sounded like a challenge to her integrity and slipped back into his arms. All, she discovered, was not much, but something prevented her from showing her disappointment. He still could not be persuaded to kiss her 'properly.' Even the most proper novels ended with the words 'Their lips met,' and Eileen asked in all innocence if he didn't like this.

'No, I like,' he assured her, 'but is not hygienical,' and added with devastating realism, 'Besides, I cannot breathe through the nose only. I think perhaps I have an obstruction.'

'You should have it out,' Eileen said.

And yet she would not mock at him as she had mocked at many a young man with far less provocation. There was a warmth and solidity in him that she had need of.

When her lover had gone, Eileen went down the wooden staircase to lock the cottage door, but was tempted out into the yard by the sweetness of the night. Houses and pavements were white under a huge moon, and the branches of *Populus alba tremula* hovered over their own inky pool of shadow on the cobblestones. A light breeze came hushing through the leaves and lifted the short hairs on Eileen's temples. She stepped into the garage to wash at the faucet with icy water before going up the stairs to bed. She felt no elation, but a great calm seemed to have descended on her, and she got into bed and slept for nine hours.

The first thing Eileen saw when she opened her eyes was Mr Belkin's portable. 'He'll have to come back for his typewriter,' she told herself, unconsciously betraying her fear that perhaps he would never come back. Had not her mother taught her it was practically fatal for a girl to give all before marriage? She spent a good part of the day at her window, and by eight o'clock began planning how to return Mr Belkin's typewriter. She was just wondering whether to take off the cover and stick a dignified note in the carriage, or get Mr Lambert to take it back to his lodging and deliver it to him without a word, when she heard a light step on the stair, a discreet knock on the door.

Mr Belkin greeted her with his usual grave courtesy, and kissed her hand, which she thought nice; nobody had ever kissed her hand before. His first words, after hanging up his coat and hat and seating himself at the hearth were, 'My footsteps were dogged all the way home last night.'

Eileen was startled. 'By Beatrice?'

'Oh, no, no!'

'Not by the police, surely!'

He beamed at her. 'By a dog! A little white doggy! She followed me all the way to your house, and when I went out she was waiting for me at the corner of the Grove. I think—she is like me, she has no home.'

Eileen went up to him and laid her head against his shoulder, happy now to receive his warm hygienic kisses on her cheek.

'You are brave girl,' he murmured. 'You trust a stranger, foreigner. I like. You shall not regret. Much money, lives of many comrades have been trusted in me, and none was lost. And you will be safe.'

'You make me feel ever so safe,' said Eileen. 'I don't know why.'

'You will always be safe with me,' he repeated, 'but when the drum of Revolution sound I shall follow it wherever I am, even if I must leave you.'

'I'll go with you. So nobody will have to leave anybody.'

'You will be revolutionary?' He smiled.

'You must tell me how,' said Eileen.

Once the news of their engagement was out, the lovers were in such a hurry to get married that many people were sure Eileen must be well on the way, though this was not the case at all. No, it was a sudden longing to live together—more powerful than any sexual drive—that made them use every spare moment of the day in searching the heights of Hampstead and Highgate for lodgings, and spend the evenings looking through the local news-sheet and underlining advertisements of rooms to let. Either would have agreed that there had not been anything inevitable in their early relations. David might have left England as suddenly as he had arrived there; Eileen might have been sent far away on war work; each might have found someone else and never met again. But now nothing, nothing must prevent their living together as man and wife in the face of the world. Every time a landlady—put off perhaps by David's thick English and Eileen's shaggy appearance—changed her mind and refused to rent them rooms half promised the day before, he was visited by wild surmises of conspiracy or anti-Semitism, and the law's delays, though only amounting to a week or two for the establishment of residence, drove him to frenzy. Would not this interval be filled with potential danger for their union? He even contemplated fleeing London and hiding in some obscure provincial town where 'they' would not be able to find him, to come back under cover of night on the eve of the day fixed for their marriage. Eileen kept looking at her pale face and insomnious eyes in shopwindows—was she going into a decline?

But nothing untoward happened. They found rooms on the top floor of a five-story house, with a view over the ponds and copses of Hampstead Heath, and were made man and wife at the Hampstead Town Hall on a day in February, 1917, when there had been no news from the Russian front for over a week. Before a month was over, the drum of Revolution sounded, and it was just as they had both said: he followed its summons and she went with him.

IVY LITVINOV

The Licorice Fields at Pontefract

In the licorice fields at Pontefract
    My love and I did meet
And many a burdened licorice bush
    Was blooming round our feet;
Red hair she had and golden skin,
Her sulky lips were shaped for sin,
Her sturdy legs were flannel-stack'd,
The strongest legs in Pontefract.

The light and dangling licorice flowers
    Gave off the sweetest smells;
From various black Victorian towers
    The Sunday evening bells
Came pealing over dales and hills
And tanneries and silent mills,
And lowly streets where country stops
And little shuttered corner shops.

She cast her blazing eyes on me
    And plucked a licorice leaf;
I was her captive slave and she
    My red-haired robber chief.
Oh love! for love I could not speak,
It left me winded, wilting, weak
And held in brown arms strong and bare
And wound with flaming ropes of hair.

JOHN BETJEMAN

Anna Karenina

This is before Levin and Kitty are engaged—quite early on in this marvellous novel.

At four o'clock that afternoon, Levin got out of the hired sleigh at the Zoological Gardens and, conscious that his heart was beating fast, went down the path leading to the ice hills and the skating rink, certain that he would find Kitty there, for he had seen the Shcherbatskys' carriage at the entrance.

It was a sunny, frosty day. At the gates there were rows of carriages, private sleighs, sleighs on hire, and policemen. Well-dressed people, their hats shining in the bright sunlight, swarmed at the entrance and along the well-swept paths between the little Russian cottages with their carved eaves; the feathery old birch trees in the gardens, their branches weighed down with snow, looked as if they had been dressed up in new festive vestments.

He walked along the path in the direction of the skating rink and kept saying to himself: 'You mustn't get excited! You must keep calm! What are you so excited about? What's the matter with you? Keep still, stupid,' he told his heart. But the more he tried to compose himself, the more breathless he became with excitement. A man he knew met and hailed him, but Levin did not even notice who it was. He went up to the ice hills, which re-sounded with the clanking of the chains by which the toboggans were being pulled up or down, their clatter as they slid down, and the sound of merry voices. He walked a few more steps, and there was the skating rink before him and he at once recognized her among the many skaters.

He knew she was there by the joy and terror that gripped his heart. She stood talking to a woman at the opposite end of the rink. There was apparently nothing striking about her dress or her attitude: but Levin found it as easy to recognize her in that crowd of people as a rose among nettles. Everything became bright in her presence. She was the smile that brightened everything around. 'Can I really go down onto the ice and go up to her?' he thought. The spot where she stood seemed to him an unapproachable sanctuary, and there was one moment when he nearly went away, so terrified was he. He had to make an effort and reason with himself that all sorts of people were walking near her and that he himself might have come to skate there. He went down, trying not to look long at her, as though she were the sun, but he saw her, as one sees the sun, without looking.

LEO TOLSTOY

Love in a Life

Room after room,
I hunt the house through
We inhabit together.
Heart, fear nothing, for, heart, thou shalt find her,
Next time, herself!—not the trouble behind her
Left in the curtain, the couch's perfume!
As she brushed it, the cornice-wreath blossomed anew,—
Yon looking-glass gleamed at the wave of her feather.

Yet the day wears,
And door succeeds door;
I try the fresh fortune—
Range the wide house from the wing to the centre.
Still the same chance! she goes out as I enter.
Spend my whole day in the quest,—who cares?
But 'tis twilight, you see,—with such suites to explore,
Such closets to search, such alcoves to importune!

ROBERT BROWNING

Lovers Infinitenesse

If yet I have not all thy love,
Deare, I shall never have it all,
I cannot breath one other sigh, to move,
Nor can intreat one other teare to fall,
And all my treasure, which should purchase thee,
Sighs, teares, and oathes, and letters I have spent.
Yet no more can be due to mee,
Than at the bargaine made was ment,
If then thy gift of love were partiall,
That some to mee, some should to others fall,
    Deare, I shall never have Thee All.

Or if then thou gavest mee all,
All was but All, which thou hadst then;
But if in thy heart, since, there be or shall,
New love created bee, by other men,
Which have their stocks intire, and can in teares,
In sighs, in oathes, and letters outbid mee,
This new love may beget new feares,
For, this love was not vowed by thee.
And yet it was, thy gift being generall,
The ground, thy heart is mine, what ever shall
    Grow there, deare, I should have it all.

Yet I would not have all yet,
Hee that hath all can have no more,
And since my love doth every day admit
New growth, thou shouldst have new rewards in
    store;
Thou canst not every day give me thy heart,
If thou canst give it, then thou never gavest it:
It stayes at home, and thou with losing savest it:
But wee will have a way more liberall,
Than changing hearts, to joyne them, so wee shall
    Be one, and one anothers All.

JOHN DONNE

Tender is the Night

Rosemary Hoyt, a very young, but already famous, film star, has met the wonderfully glamorous couple, Nicole and Dick Diver, on holiday in the South of France. There are two separate excerpts here; both from early in the book.

For a moment now she was beside Dick Diver on the path. Alongside his hard, neat brightness everything faded into the surety that he knew everything. For a year, which was for ever, she had had money and a certain celebrity and contact with the celebrated, and these latter had presented themselves merely as powerful enlargements of the people with whom the doctor's widow and her daughter had associated in a hôtel-pension in Paris. Rosemary was a romantic and her career had not provided many satisfactory opportunities on that score. Her mother, with the idea of a career for Rosemary, would not tolerate any such spurious substitutes as the excitations available on all sides, and indeed Rosemary was already beyond that—she was In the movies but not at all At them. So when she had seen approval of Dick Diver in her mother's face it meant that he was 'the real thing'; it meant permission to go as far as she could.

'I was watching you,' he said, and she knew he meant it. 'We've grown very fond of you.'

'I fell in love with you the first time I saw you,' she said quietly.

He pretended not to have heard, as if the compliment were purely formal.

'New friends,' he said, as if it were an important point, 'can often have a better time together than old friends.'

With that remark, which she did not understand precisely, she found herself at the table, picked out by slowly emerging lights against the dark dusk. A chord of delight struck inside her when she saw that Dick had taken her mother on his right hand; for herself she was between Luis Campion and Brady.

Surcharged with her emotion she turned to Brady with the intention of confiding in him, but at her first mention of Dick a hard-boiled sparkle in his eyes gave her to understand that he refused the fatherly office. In turn she was equally firm when he tried to monopolize her hand, so they talked shop or rather she listened while he talked shop, her polite eyes never leaving his face, but her mind was so definitely elsewhere that she felt he must guess the fact. Intermittently she caught the gist of his sentences and supplied the rest from her subconscious, as one picks up the striking of a clock in the middle with only the rhythm of the first uncounted strokes lingering in the mind.

The semi-booth gave on the *vestiaire* and as Rosemary hung up the receiver she heard two low voices not five feet from her on the other side of a row of coats.

'—So you love me?'

'Oh, *do* I!'

It was Nicole—Rosemary hesitated in the door of the booth—then she heard Dick say:

'I want you terribly—let's go to the hotel now.' Nicole gave a little gasping sigh. For a moment the words conveyed nothing at all to Rosemary—but the tone did. The vast secretiveness of it vibrated to herself.

'I want you.'

'I'll be at the hotel at four.'

Rosemary stood breathless as the voices moved away. She was at first even astonished—she had seen them in their relation to each other as people without personal exigencies—as something cooler. Now a strong current of emotion flowed through her, profound and unidentified. She did not know whether she was attracted or repelled, but only that she was deeply moved. It made her feel very alone as she went back into the restaurant, but it was touching to look in upon, and the passionate gratitude of Nicole's 'Oh *do* I!' echoed in her mind. The particular mood of the passage she had witnessed lay ahead of her; but however far she was from it her stomach told her it was all right—she had none of the aversion she had felt in the playing of certain love scenes in pictures.

F. SCOTT FITZGERALD

The Owl and The Pussy Cat

The Owl and the Pussy-Cat went to sea
   In a beautiful pea-green boat.
They took some honey, and plenty of money
   Wrapped up in a five-pound note.
The Owl looked up to the stars above,
   And sang to a small guitar,
'O lovely Pussy! O Pussy, my love,
What a beautiful Pussy you are,
      You are,
      You are!
What a beautiful Pussy you are!'

Pussy said to the Owl, 'You elegant fowl!
   How charmingly sweet you sing!
O let us be married! too long we have tarried:
   But what shall we do for a ring?'
They sailed away, for a year and a day,
   To the land where the Bong-Tree grows,
And there in a wood a Piggy-wig stood,
With a ring at the end of his nose,
      His nose,
      His nose!
With a ring at the end of his nose.

'Dear Pig, are you willing to sell for one shilling
    Your ring?' Said the Piggy, 'I will.'
So they took it away, and were married next day
    By the Turkey who lives on the hill.
They dinèd on mince, and slices of quince,
    Which they ate with a runcible spoon;
And hand in hand, on the edge of the sand
    They danced by the light of the moon,
        The moon,
        The moon,
They danced by the light of the moon.

EDWARD LEAR

The Charterhouse of Parma

Count Mosca is married, but passionately in love with a Contessa far younger than himself. She, however, returns his love: their problem is how they can spend most time together. Here are his proposals to her.

At the degree of intimacy which in Italy follows on love there was no longer any obstacle in the nature of vanity between the two lovers. It was therefore with the most perfect simplicity that Mosca said to the woman he adored: 'I have two or three plans of conduct to offer you, all of them fairly well thought out. I have been pondering over nothing else for the past three months. First: I hand in my resignation and we go to live as good plain folk in Milan, Florence, Naples, or wherever you please. We have an income of 15,000 lire, apart from what we receive from the Prince's liberality, which will continue for some time, more or less. Secondly: You condescend to come to the place in which I have some influence. You buy a property, Sacca, for example, a charming house in the middle of a forest overlooking the river Po; you can have the contract signed within a week from now. The Prince will attach you to his court. But here I can see an enormous obstacle. You will be well received at court; nobody would presume to jib at this when I am there. Besides, the Princess imagines she is unhappy, and I have recently rendered her certain services with a view to your interest. But I must remind you of a paramount objection: the Prince is an extremely bigoted churchman, and, as you already know, as luck will have it I am a married man. From this will arise a million minor unpleasantnesses. You are a widow; that is a fine title that should be exchanged for another, and this forms the subject of my third proposal.

'One might find you a new husband who would not be too much in the way. But first of all he would have to be considerably advanced in years, for why should you deny me the hope of succeeding him one day? Well now, I have arranged this curious business with the Duca Sanseverina-Taxis, who, of course does not know the name of his future Duchessa. He knows only that she will make him an ambassador and will procure him the Grand Cordon which his father had, and the lack of which makes him the unhappiest of mortals. Apart from this, the Duca is not too much of a fool. He gets his clothes and his wigs from Paris; he is not in the least the sort of man to do anything deliberately spiteful, he seriously believes that honour consists in having a Cordon, and he is ashamed of his wealth. He came to me a year ago to suggest his founding a hospital, in order to get this Cordon. I laughed at him then, but he did not by any means laugh at me when I proposed a marriage to him. My first condition was, of course, that he should never set foot again in Parma.'

'But do you know that what you are proposing to me is highly immoral?' said the Contessa.

'No more immoral than everything else that is done at our court and a score of others. Absolute power has this advantage, that it sanctifies everything in the eyes of the public, and what thing can be absurd when nobody notices it? Our policy for the next twenty years is going to consist in feeling fear of the Jacobins— and what fear, too! Every year, we shall fancy ourselves on the eve of '93. You will hear, I hope, the fine speeches I make on that subject at my receptions! They are beautiful! Anything that can in some slight way reduce this fear will be *supremely moral* in the eyes of the nobles and the bigots. And in Parma, as it happens, everyone who is not either a noble or a bigot is in prison, or packing up to go there. You may rest assured that this marriage will not seem out of the ordinary at our court until the day on which I fall out of favour. This arrangement involves no dishonest trick on anyone; that, so it seems to me, is the essential thing. The Prince, on whose favour we are trading, has placed only one condition on his consent, which is that the future Duchessa shall be of noble birth. Last year my office, all told, brought me in 107,000 lire; my total income must have been 122,000; I invested 20,000 at Lyons.

'Well then, make your choice: either, a life of luxury based on our having 122,000 lire to spend, which, in Parma, will go at least as far as 400,000 in Milan; but with this marriage which will give you the name of a passable man whom you will never see once you leave the altar; or else a modest, comfortable existence on 15,000 lire in Florence or Naples, for I agree with you that you have been too much admired in Milan. Envy would make our lives a burden there, and that might possibly finish by souring our tempers. The splendid existence we shall lead in Parma will, I hope, have some touches of novelty, even in your eyes which have seen the court of Prince Eugène. You would be wise to become acquainted with it before shutting the door upon it. Don't think that I am trying to influence your opinion. As for me, my own choice is quite clear: I would rather live on a fourth floor with you than continue that grand existence by myself.'

STENDHAL

Songs from The Old Wife's Tale

(1)

When as the rye reach to the chin,
And chopcherry, chopcherry ripe within,
Strawberries swimming in the cream,
And school-boys playing in the stream;
    Then O, then O, then O my true love said,
      Till that time come again,
    She could not live a maid.

Lo! here we come a-reaping, a-reaping,
To reap our harvest fruit,
And thus we pass the years so long,
　　And never be we mute.

A Voice Speaks from the Well

Fair maiden, white and red,
Comb me smooth, and stroke my head;
And thou shalt have some cockle bread.
Gently dip, but not too deep,
For fear thou make the golden beard to weep.
Fair maid, white and red,
Comb me smooth, and stroke my head;
And every hair a sheave shall be,
And every sheave a golden tree.

GEORGE PEELE

Going to Bed

Come, madam, come, all rest my powers defy;
Until I labour, I in labour lie.
The foe ofttimes, having the foe in sight,
Is tired with standing, though he never fight.
Off with that girdle, like heaven's zone glittering,
But a far fairer world encompassing.
Unpin that spangled breast-plate, which you wear,
That th'eyes of busy fools may be stopp'd there.
Unlace yourself, for that harmonious chime
Tells me from you that now it is bed-time.
Off with that happy busk, which I envy,
That still can be, and still can stand so nigh.
Your gown going off such beauteous state reveals,

As when from flowery meads th'hill's shadow steals.
Off with your wiry coronet, and show
The hairy diadems which on you do grow.
Off with your hose and shoes; then softly tread
In this love's hallow'd temple, this soft bed.
In such white robes heaven's angels used to be
Revealed to men; thou, angel, bring'st with thee
A heaven-like Mahomet's paradise; and though
Ill spirits walk in white, we easily know
By this these angels from an evil sprite;
Those set our hairs, but these our flesh upright.
     Licence my roving hands, and let them go
Before, behind, between, above, below.
Oh, my America, my Newfoundland,
My kingdom, safest when with one man mann'd,
My mine of precious stones, my empery;
How am I blest in thus discovering thee!
To enter in these bonds, is to be free;
Then, where my hand is set, my seal shall be.
     Full nakedness! All joys are due to thee;
As souls unbodied, bodies unclothed must be
To taste whole joys. Gems which you women use
Are like Atlanta's ball cast in men's views;
That, when a fool's eye lighteth on a gem,
His earthly soul might court that, not them.
Like pictures, or like books' gay coverings made
For laymen, are all women thus array'd.
Themselves are only mystic books, which we
—Whom their imputed grace will dignify—
Must see reveal'd. Then, since that I may know,
As liberally as to thy midwife show
Thyself; cast all, yea, this white linen hence;
There is no penance due to innocence:
     To teach thee, I am naked first; why than,
What needst thou have more covering than a man?

JOHN DONNE

Everything in Common
(from Table Talk)

Between husband and wife there should be no question as to *meum* and *tuum*. All things should be in common between them, without any distinction or means of distinguishing.

MARTIN LUTHER

Back

This is the end of Henry Green's penultimate novel, when the shell-shocked hero, who has lost one girl, joins the woman he is to marry.

So she had asked him to marry her, and had been accepted. She had made only one condition, which was that they should have a trial trip. So it was the same night, under Mr Mandrew's roof, that he went to her room, for the first time in what was to be a happy married life.

She was lying stark naked on the bed, a lamp with a pink shade at her side. She had not drawn the blackout, and the electric light made the dark outside a marvellous deep blue. In an attempt to seem natural, he said something about showing a light.

'Come here, silly,' was what she replied.

Then he knelt by the bed, having under his eyes the great, the overwhelming sight of the woman he loved, for the first time without her clothes. And because the lamp was lit, the pink shade seemed to spill a light of roses over her in all their summer colours, her hands that lay along her legs were red, her stomach gold, her breasts the colour of cream roses, and her neck white roses for the bride. She had shut her eyes to let him have his fill, but it was too much, for he burst into tears again, he buried his face in her side just below the ribs, and bawled like a child. 'Rose,' he called out, not knowing he did so, 'Rose.'

'There,' Nancy said, 'there,' pressed his head with her hands. His tears wetted her. The salt water ran down between her legs.

And she knew what she had taken on. It was no more or less, really, than she had expected.

HENRY GREEN

Green Heart

Cromyomancy carves out a preview
And a foretaste of you:
Brittle as gold-leaf the outer skin,
Firmness within;
Full savour, more piercing than any
Peach or strawberry;
The heart will grow.

From the beginning, tears flow,
But of no rage or grief:
Wise cromyomancers know
Weeping augurs belief.

KINGSLEY AMIS

cromyomancy: divination by means of onions.

Part IV

ANGUISH, GRIEF, PARTINGS
JEALOUSY, DEATH

No shortage of material here—rather a sea of troubles, a rich crop of distress. One of the facts that emerges is that, in love, it is women who lose and suffer most. Byron's famous remark from *Don Juan:* 'Man's love is of man's life a thing apart/ 'Tis woman's whole existence;' may no longer be strictly, or even at all, true; nonetheless, if an anthology ranges over the last five hundred years, there is bound to be a good deal of that sort of thing. And *has* the situation changed so much in this respect? Look at the excerpt from *The Deep Blue Sea* by Rattigan; or at *The Willow Cabin* by Pamela Frankau, or at *The Pursuit of Love.* All of these works are under twenty-five years old; all are about women whose lives are over-whelmed by their love for men who are, respectively, emotionally immature and unable to respond, or indifferent, or who die, or who are morally forbidden. When men feel as much for women (in fiction, at least) the women simply die: Knut Hamsun's *Victoria* and Hemingway's *A Farewell To Arms* are examples here. It is true that women have evolved to the point where they are able to have many kinds of far lighter relationships with men while retaining their professions, their work, their independent and separate lives, but when it comes to the serious, whole-hearted love, I don't think the situation has changed very much. That cannot really change until men get around to feeling that it would be worth *their* while to change. The trouble is that of those who lose the world for love, few can count it well lost, as so few *couples* (one person will not do here) are able to recognise that love, like every-thing else connected with life and particularly human life, has to be perpetually on the move in order to sustain itself.

We are far more like children who say, 'look what I've found!' as we enclose a bird's egg or a butterfly in the boiling palm of our hand and expose it a few seconds later in smithereens.

Men write extremely well about what it feels like to be a woman abandoned or betrayed by a lover. Byron, as we have said, C. Day Lewis with a savagely perceptive poem 'The Mirror', Shakespeare (can one *count* Shakespeare, as, like Anon, there is nothing he cannot do?) and the afore-mentioned Terence Rattigan and Hamsun. Graves's poem 'The Presence' is the best example I have found of a man in anguish from a separation, but I have also included a letter of Hazlitt's, depicting his agony about Sarah Walker. Muriel Stuart's poem reproduces one of the bitter and classic ends of a love affair—what is deadly earnest for the woman is deadly fun for the man. There are some very touching letters of farewell, letters of love and the agony of separation written by semi-literates who move one more because their need to express themselves has transcended their incapacity. This part shows, more than any other, how much we prize the *idea* of loving, and how much each person needs to love and to be loved.

Contents

In the Orchard

'I thought you loved me.' 'No, it was only fun.'
'When we stood there, closer than all?' 'Well, the harvest
   moon
Was shining and queer in your hair, and it turned my head.'
'That made you?' 'Yes.' 'Just the room and the light it
   made
Under the tree?' 'Well, your mouth, too.' 'Yes, my mouth?'
'And the quiet there that sang like the drum in the booth.
You shouldn't have danced like that.' 'Like what?' 'So
   close,
With your head turned up, and the flower in your hair, a
   rose
That smelt all warm.' 'I loved you. I thought you knew
I wouldn't have danced like that with any but you.'
'I didn't know. I thought you knew it was fun.'
'I thought it was love you meant.' 'Well, it's done.' 'Yes,
   it's done.
I've seen boys stone a blackbird, and watched them drown
A kitten . . . it clawed at the reeds, and they pushed it
   down
Into the pool while it screamed. Is that fun, too?'
'Well, boys are like that . . . Your brothers . . .' 'Yes, I
   know.
But you, so lovely and strong! Not you! Not you!'
'They don't understand it's cruel. It's only a game.'
'And are girls fun, too?' 'No, still in a way it's the same.
It's queer and lovely to have a girl . . .' 'Go on.'
'It makes you mad for a bit to feel she's your own,
And you laugh and kiss her, and maybe you give her a ring,
But it's only in fun.' 'But I gave you everything.'
'Well, you shouldn't have done it. You know what a
   fellow thinks
When a girl does that.' 'Yes, he talks of her over his drinks
And calls her a—' 'Stop that now. I thought you knew.'
'But it wasn't with anyone else. It was only you.'
'How did I know? I thought you wanted it too.

137

I thought you were like the rest. Well, what's to be done?'
'To be done?' 'Is it all right?' 'Yes.' 'Sure?' 'Yes, but why?'
'I don't know. I thought you were going to cry.
You said you had something to tell me.' 'Yes, I know.
It wasn't anything really . . . I think I'll go.'
'Yes, it's late. There's thunder about, a drop of rain
Fell on my hand in the dark. I'll see you again
At the dance next week. You're sure that everything's right?'
'Yes.' 'Well, I'll be going.' 'Kiss me . . .' 'Good night.' . . .
   'Good night.'

MURIEL STUART

Sir Walter Ralegh to Lady Elizabeth Ralegh (1603)

You shall now receive (my deare wife) my last words in these
my last lines. My love I send you that you may keep it when I am
dead, and my councell that you may remember it when I am no
more. I would not by my will present you with sorrowes (dear
Besse) let them go to the grave with me and be buried in the dust.
And seeing that it is not Gods will that I should see you any more
in this life, beare it patiently, and with a heart like thy selfe.

First, I send you all the thankes which my heart can conceive, or
my words can reherse for your many travailes, and care taken for
me, which though they have not taken effect as you wished, yet
my debt to you is not the lesse: but pay it I never shall in this
world.

Secondly, I beseech you for the love you beare me living, do not
hide your selfe many dayes, but by your travailes seeke to helpe
your miserable fortunes and the right of your poor childe. Thy
mourning cannot availe me, I am but dust.

Thirdly, you shall understand, that my land was conveyed *bona
fide* to my childe; the writings were drawne at midsummer was
twelve months, my honest cosen Brett can testify so much, and
Dolberry too, can remember somewhat therein. And I trust my
blood will quench their malice that have cruelly murthered me:
and that they will not seek also to kill thee and thine with extreame
poverty.

To what friend to direct thee I know not, for all mine have left me in the true time of tryall. And I perceive that my death was determined from the first day. Most sorry I am God knowes that being thus surprised with death I can leave you in no better estate. God is my witnesse I meant you all my office of wines or all that I could have purchased by selling it, halfe of my stuffe, and all my jewels, but some one for the boy, but God hath prevented all my resolutions. That great God that ruleth all in all, but if you live free from want, care for no more, for the rest is but vanity. Love God, and begin betimes to repose your selfe upon him, and therein shall you finde true and lasting riches, and endlesse comfort: for the rest when you have travailed and wearied your thoughts over all sorts of worldly cogitations, you shall but sit downe by sorrowe in the end.

Teach your son also to love and feare God while he is yet young, that the feare of God may grow with him, and then God will be a husband to you, and a father to him; a husband and a father which cannot be taken from you.

Baily oweth me 200 pounds, and Adrian Gilbert 600. In Jersey I also have much owing me besides. The arrearages of the wines will pay my debts. And howsoever you do, for my soules sake, pay all poore men. When I am gone, no doubt you shall be sought for by many, for the world thinkes that I was very rich. But take heed of the pretences of men, and their affections, for they last not but in honest and worthy men, and no greater misery can befall you in this life, than to become a prey, and afterwards to be despised. I speake not this (God knowes) to dissuade you from marriage, for it will be best for you, both in respect of the world and of God. As for me, I am no more yours, nor you mine, death hath cut us asunder: and God hath divided me from the world, and you from me.

Remember your poor childe for his father's sake, who chose you, and loved you in his happiest times. Get those letters (if it be possible) which I writ to the Lords, wherein I sued for my life: God is my witnesse it was for you and yours that I desired life, but it is true that I disdained my self for begging of it: for know it (my deare wife) that your son is the son of a true man, and one who in his owne respect despiseth death and all his misshapen & ugly formes.

I cannot write much, God he knows how hardly I steale this time while others sleep, and it is also time that I should separate my thoughts from the world. Begg my dead body which living was denied thee; and either lay it at Sherburne (and if the land continue) or in Exeter-Church, by my Father and Mother; I can say no more, time and death call me away.

The everlasting God, powerfull, infinite, and omnipotent God, That Almighty God, who is goodnesse it selfe, the true life and true light keep thee and thine: have mercy on me, and teach me to forgive my persecutors and false accusers, and send us to meet in his glorious Kingdome. My deare wife farewell. Blesse my poore boy. Pray for me, and let my good God hold you both in his armes.

Written with the dying hand of sometimes thy Husband, but now alasse overthrowne.

Yours that was, but now not my own.
Walter Rawleigh

Remembrance

They flee from me, that sometime did me seek
   With naked foot, stalking in my chamber.
I have seen them gentle, tame, and meek,
   That now are wild, and do not remember
   That sometime they put themselves in danger
     To take bread at my hand; and now they range
     Busily seeking with a continual change.

Thanked be fortune it hath been otherwise
   Twenty times better; but once, in special,
In thin array, after a pleasant guise,
   When her loose gown from her shoulders did fall,
   And she me caught in her arms long and small,
     Therewith all sweetly did me kiss
     And softly said, 'Dear heart how like you this?'

It was no dream; I lay broad waking:
    But all is turned, thorough my gentleness,
Into a strange fashion of forsaking;
    And I have leave to go of her goodness,
    And she also to use newfangleness.
        But since that I so kindly am served,
        I would fain know what she hath deserved.

SIR THOMAS WYATT

The Deep Blue Sea

Hester Collyer has left her kind and successful husband to go and live with Freddie Page, an ex-RAF pilot with whom she is desperately in love. Collyer has come to see her, because she had tried to kill herself. She has made it clear to him that she will not return to him.

Act I

. . . .

HESTER: I could always impress your erudite friends, when put to it. I only wish I were as good with Freddie's friends.
COLLYER: Aren't you?
HESTER: Oh no. On pub crawls I'm a terrible fish out of water.
COLLYER: Pub crawls?
HESTER: Oh, you needn't be shocked. There's nothing in the world more respectable than pub crawls. More respectable or more unspeakably dreary.
Pause.
COLLYER: Hester—
HESTER: Yes?
COLLYER: It doesn't matter. The question I was going to ask you is too big to put into a single sentence.

HESTER: (*Slowly*) Perhaps the answer could be put into a single word.

COLLYER: We might disagree on the choice of that word.

HESTER: I don't expect so. There are polite words and impolite words. They all add up to the same emotion. (*Pointing to a picture.*) That's my latest.

COLLYER: Very nice. What were you angry with Page about?

HESTER: Oh, lots of things. Always the same things.

COLLYER: What?

HESTER: That word we were talking about just now. Shall we call it love? It saves a lot of trouble.

COLLYER: You said just now his feelings for you hadn't changed.

HESTER: They haven't, Bill. They couldn't, you see. Zero minus zero is still zero.

Pause. COLLYER *pushes her away from him to look into her eyes.*

COLLYER: How long have you known this?

HESTER: From the beginning.

COLLYER: But you told me—

HESTER: I don't know what I told you, Bill. If I lied, I'm sorry. You must blame my conventional upbringing. You see I was brought up to think that in a case of this kind it's more proper for it to be the man who does the loving.

Pause.

COLLYER: But how, in the name of reason, could you have gone on loving a man who, by your own confession, can give you nothing in return?

HESTER: Oh, but he can give me something in return, and even does, from time to time.

COLLYER: What?

HESTER: Himself.

COLLYER *stares at her. There is a pause.*

COLLYER: Perhaps you're right, Hester. Perhaps there is no one who can help you.

HESTER: (*Mockingly*) Except myself, you were going to say.

COLLYER: Yes, I was.

HESTER: I thought you were.

And here is Hester with Freddie in the last scene of the second act. In the original production these parts were unforgettably played by Dame Peggy Ashcroft and Kenneth More.

Act II

HESTER *closes the door behind him and then goes quickly to the bedroom door. She knocks.*

HESTER: (*Calling.*) Freddie, let me in, darling.

There is no answer. She knocks again.

Freddie—don't be childish. Let me in.

There is no answer. HESTER *walks away from the door and goes to get a cigarette. As she is lighting it* FREDDIE *emerges from the bedroom. He has changed into a blue suit.*

Why, Freddie, you're looking very smart. Going out somewhere?

FREDDIE: Yes.

HESTER: Where?

FREDDIE: To see a man about a job.

HESTER: What man?

FREDDIE: Lopez. I've just called him.

HESTER: Lopez?

FREDDIE: The South American I had lunch with.

HESTER: Oh yes, of course. I'd forgotten. How did it go off?

FREDDIE: It went off all right.

HESTER: Oh good. You think you'll get the job?

FREDDIE: Yes, I think so. He made a fairly definite offer. Of course it's up to his boss.

HESTER: Let's have a look at you. (*She inspects him.*) Oh, darling, you might have changed your shirt.

FREDDIE: Well, I hadn't a clean one.

HESTER: No. Nor you had. The laundry's late again this week. I'll wash one out for you to-morrow.

FREDDIE: Yes. Does it look too bad?

HESTER: No. It'll pass. Your shoes need a clean.

FREDDIE: Yes. I'll give them a rub.

HESTER: No. Take them off. I'll do them. (*She goes towards the kitchen.*) Somehow or other you always manage to get shoe polish over your face—Lord knows how.

She disappears into the kitchen. FREDDIE *takes his shoes off.* HESTER *comes back with shoe brushes and a tin of polish. She takes the shoes from him and begins to clean them. There is a fairly long silence.*

What's the job?

FREDDIE: (*Muttering.*) Yes. I suppose I must tell you.

HESTER *gives him a quick glance.*

143

HESTER: Yes, Freddie. I think I'd like to know.

FREDDIE: Look, Hes. I've got to talk for a bit now. It's not going to be easy, so don't interrupt, do you mind? You always could argue the hind leg off a donkey—and just when I've got things clear in my mind I don't want them muddled up again.

HESTER: I'm sorry, Freddie. I must interrupt at once. The way you've been behaving this afternoon, how could you have things clear in your mind?

FREDDIE: I'm all right now, Hes. I had a cup of black coffee and after that a bit of a walk. I know what I'm doing.

HESTER: And what are you doing, Freddie?

FREDDIE: Accepting a job in South America as a test pilot.

HESTER: Test pilot? But you've said a hundred times you could never go back to that. After that crash in Canada you told me you had no nerve or judgment left.

FREDDIE: They'll come back. I had too many drinks that time in Canada. You know that.

HESTER: Yes, I know that. So did the Court of Inquiry know that. Does this man Lopez know that?

FREDDIE: No, of course not. He won't hear either. Don't worry about my nerve and judgment, Hes. A month or two on the wagon and I'll be the old ace again—the old dicer with death.

HESTER: (*Sharply.*) Don't use that idiotic RAF slang, Freddie. (*More gently.*) Do you mind? This is too important—

FREDDIE: Yes. It is important.

HESTER: Whereabouts in South America?

FREDDIE: Somewhere near Rio.

HESTER: I see. (*She continues to clean the shoes mechanically.*) Well, when do we start?

FREDDIE: We don't.

HESTER: We don't?

FREDDIE: You and I don't. That's what I'm trying to tell you. I'm going alone.

HESTER *lays the shoe down quietly, staring at* FREDDIE.

HESTER: (*At length.*) Why, Freddie?

FREDDIE: If I'm to stay on the wagon, I've got to be alone.

HESTER: (*In a near whisper.*) Have you?

FREDDIE: Oh hell—that's not the real reason. Listen, Hes, darling.

There is a pause while he paces the room as if concentrating desperately on finding the words. HESTER *watches him.*

You've always said, haven't you, that I don't really love you?

144

Well, I suppose, in your sense I don't. But what I do feel for you is a good deal stronger than I've ever felt for anybody else in my life, or ever will feel, I should think. That's why I went away with you in the first place, that's why I've stayed with you all this time, and that's why I must go away from you now.

HESTER: (*At length.*) That sounds rather like a prepared speech, Freddie.

FREDDIE: Yes. I suppose it is a bit prepared. I worked it out on my walk. But it's still true, Hes. I'm too fond of you to let things slide. That letter was a hell of a shock. I knew often you were unhappy—you often knew I was a bit down too. But I hadn't a clue how much the—difference in our feelings had been hurting you. It's asking too damn' much of any bloke to go on as if nothing had happened when he knows now for a fact that he's driving the only girl he's ever loved to suicide.

HESTER: (*In a low voice.*) Do you think your leaving me will drive me away from suicide?

FREDDIE: (*Simply.*) That's a risk I shall just have to take, isn't it? It's a risk both of us will have to face.

Pause.

HESTER: Freddie—you mustn't scare me like this.

FREDDIE: No scare, Hes. Sorry, this is on the level.

HESTER: You know perfectly well you'll feel quite differently in the morning.

FREDDIE: No, I won't, Hes. Not this time. Besides I don't think I'll be here in the morning.

HESTER: Where will you be?

FREDDIE: I don't know. Somewhere. I think I'd better get out to-night.

HESTER: No, Freddie. No.

FREDDIE: It's better that way. I'm scared of your arguing. *Passionately.*) I know this is right, you see. I know it, but with your gift of the gab, you'll muddle things up for me again, and I'll be lost.

HESTER: I won't, Freddie. I won't. I promise I won't. But you must stay to-night. Just to-night.

FREDDIE: (*Unhappily.*) No, Hes.

HESTER: Just to-night, Freddie. Only one night.

FREDDIE: No. Sorry, Hes.

HESTER: Don't be so cruel, Freddie. How can you be so cruel?

FREDDIE: Hes—this is our last chance. If we miss it, we're done for. We're death to each other, you and I.

HESTER: That isn't true.

FREDDIE: It is true, darling, and you've known it longer than I have. I'm such a damn' fool and that's been the trouble, or I should have done this long ago. That's it, you know. It's written in great bloody letters of fire over our heads—'You and I are death to each other'.

HESTER *is unrestrainedly weeping.*

FREDDIE *comes over to her and picks up his shoes.*

HESTER: I haven't finished them.

FREDDIE: They're all right. (*He begins to put them on.*) I'm sorry. Hes. Oh God, I'm sorry. Please don't cry. You don't know what it does to me.

HESTER: Not now. Not this minute. Not this minute, Freddie?

FREDDIE *finishes putting on his shoes, and then turns away from her, brushing his sleeve across his eyes.*

HESTER: (*Going to him.*) You've got all your things here. You've got to pack—

FREDDIE: I'll send for them.

HESTER: You promised to come back for dinner.

FREDDIE: I know. I'm sorry about that. (*He kisses her quickly and goes to the door.*)

HESTER: (*Frantically.*) But you can't break a promise like that, Freddie. You can't. Come back just for our dinner, Freddie. I won't argue, I swear, and then if you want to go away afterwards—

FREDDIE *goes out.* HESTER *runs to the door after him.*

Freddie, come back. . . . Don't go. . . . Don't leave me alone to-night. . . . Not to-night. . . . Don't leave me alone to-night. . . .

She has followed him out as the CURTAIN *falls.*

TERENCE RATTIGAN

A New Courtly Sonnet of the Lady Greensleeves

Greensleeves was all my joy,
Greensleeves was my delight;
Greensleeves was my heart of gold,
And who but Lady Greensleeves.

Alas, my Love! ye do me wrong
   To cast me off discourteously;
And I have loved you so long,
   Delighting in your company.
      Greensleeves was all my joy, &c.

I have been ready at your hand,
   To grant whatever you would crave;
I have both waged life and land,
   Your love and goodwill for to have.
      Greensleeves was all my joy, &c.

I bought thee kerchers to thy head,
   That were wrought fine and gallantly;
I kept thee both at board and bed,
   Which cost my purse well favouredly.
      Greensleeves was all my joy, &c.

I bought thee petticoats of the best,
   The cloth so fine as fine might be;
I gave thee jewels for thy chest,
   And all this cost I spent on thee.
      Greensleeves was all my joy, &c.

Thy smock of silk, both fair and white,
   With gold embroidered gorgeously;
Thy petticoat of sendal right;
   And thus I bought thee gladly.
      Greensleeves was all my joy, &c.

Thy girdle of gold so red,
   With pearls bedecked sumptuously;
The like no other lasses had,
   And yet thou wouldst not love me.
      Greensleeves was all my joy, &c.

Thy purse and eke thy gay gilt knives,
   Thy pincase gallant to the eye;
No better wore the burgess wives,
   And yet thou wouldst not love me.
      Greensleeves was all my joy, &c.

Thy crimson stockings all of silk,
   With gold all wrought above the knee;
Thy pumps as white as was the milk,
   And yet thou wouldst not love me.
      Greensleeves was all my joy, &c.

Thy gown was of the grassy green,
   Thy sleeves of satin hanging by,
Which made thee be our harvest queen,
   And yet thou wouldst not love me.
      Greensleeves was all my joy, &c.

Thy garters fringed with the gold,
   And silver aglets hanging by,
Which made thee blithe for to behold,
   And yet thou wouldst not love me.
      Greensleeves was all my joy, &c.

My gayest gelding I thee gave,
   To ride wherever liked thee;
No lady ever was so brave,
   And yet thou wouldst not love me.
      Greensleeves was all my joy, &c.

My men were clothed all in green,
   And they did ever wait on thee;
All this was gallant to be seen,
   And yet thou wouldst not love me.
      Greensleeves was all my joy, &c

They set thee up, they took thee down,
   They served thee with humility;
Thy foot might not once touch the ground,
   And yet thou wouldst not love me.
      Greensleeves was all my joy, &c.

For every morning when thou rose,
   I sent thee dainties orderly,
To cheer thy stomach from all woes,
   And yet thou wouldst not love me.
      Greensleeves was all my joy, &c.

Thou couldst desire no earthly thing
   But still thou hadst it readily;
Thy music still to play and sing,
   And yet thou wouldst not love me.
      Greensleeves was all my joy, &c.

And who did pay for all this gear
   That thou didst spend when pleased thee?
Even I that am rejected here,
   And thou disdain'st to love me.
      Greensleeves was all my joy, &c.

Well, I will pray to God on high,
   That thou my constancy mayst see,
And that yet once before I die,
   Thou wilt vouchsafe to love me.
      Greensleeves was all my joy, &c.

Greensleeves, now farewell! adieu!
   God I pray to prosper thee;
For I am still thy lover true.
   Come once again and love me.
      Greensleeves was all my joy, &c.

ANON

The Mound

For a moment pause:—
Just here it was;
And through the thin thorn hedge, by the rays of the moon,
I can see the tree in the field, and beside it the mound—
Now sheeted with snow—whereon we sat that June
When it was green and round,
And she crazed my mind by what she coolly told—
The history of her undoing,
(As I saw it), but she called 'comradeship,'
That bred in her no rueing:
And saying she'd not be bound
For life to one man, young, ripe-yeared, or old,
Left me—an innocent simpleton to her viewing;
For, though my accompt of years outscored her own,
Hers had more hotly flown . . .
We never met again by this green mound,
To press as once so often lip on lip,
And palter, and pause:—
Yes; here it was!

THOMAS HARDY

Love Without Hope

Love without hope, as when the young bird-catcher
Swept off his tall hat to the Squire's own daughter,
So let the imprisoned larks escape and fly
Singing about her head, as she rode by.

ROBERT GRAVES

Persuasion

This is the first meeting between Ann Elliot and Captain Wentworth since she reluctantly refused him eight years earlier.

The morning hours at the Cottage were always later than those at the other house; and on the morrow the difference was so great, that Mary and Anne were not more than beginning breakfast when Charles came in to say that they were just setting off, that he was come for his dogs, that his sisters were following with Captain Wentworth, his sisters meaning to visit Mary and the child, and Captain Wentworth proposing also to wait on her for a few minutes, if not inconvenient; and though Charles had answered for the child's being in no such state as could make it inconvenient, Captain Wentworth would not be satisfied without his running on to give notice.

Mary, very much gratified by this attention, was delighted to receive him; while a thousand feelings rushed on Anne, of which this was the most consoling, that it would soon be over. And it was soon over. In two minutes after Charles's preparation, the others appeared; they were in the drawing-room. Her eye half met Captain Wentworth's; a bow, a courtesy passed; she heard his voice—he talked to Mary; said all that was right; said something to the Miss Musgroves, enough to mark an easy footing: the room seemed full—full of persons and voices—but a few minutes ended it. Charles showed himself at the window, all was ready, their visitor had bowed and was gone; the Miss Musgroves were gone too; suddenly resolving to walk to the end of the village with the sportsmen: the room was cleared, and Anne might finish her breakfast as she could.

'It is over! it is over!' she repeated to herself again and again, in nervous gratitude. 'The worst is over!'

Mary talked, but she could not attend. She had seen him. They had met. They had been once more in the same room.

Soon, however, she began to reason with herself, and try to be feeling less. Eight years, almost eight years had passed, since all had been given up. How absurd to be resuming the agitation which such an interval had banished into distance and indistinctness! What might not eight years do? Events of every description, changes, alienations, removals,—all, all must be comprised in it; and oblivion of the past—how natural how certain too! It included nearly a third part of her own life.

Alas! with all her reasonings, she found that to retentive feelings eight years may be little more than nothing.

Now, how were his sentiments to be read? Was this like wishing to avoid her? And the next moment she was hating herself for the folly which asked the question.

On one other question, which perhaps her utmost wisdom might not have prevented, she was soon spared all suspense, for after the Miss Musgroves had returned and finished their visit at the Cottage, she had this spontaneous information from Mary—

'Captain Wentworth is not very gallant by you, Anne, though he was so attentive to me. Henrietta asked him what he thought of you, when they went away; and he said, "You were so altered he should not have known you again."'

Mary had no feelings to make her respect her sister's in a common way; but she was perfectly unsuspicious of being inflicting any peculiar wound.

'Altered beyond his knowledge!' Anne fully submitted, in silent, deep mortification. Doubtless it was so; and she could take no revenge, for he was not altered, or not for the worse. She had already acknowledged it to herself, and she could not think differently, let him think of her as he would. No; the years which had destroyed her youth and bloom had only given him a more glowing, manly, open look, in no respect lessening his personal advantages. She had seen the same Frederick Wentworth.

'So altered that he should not have known her again!' These were words which could not but dwell with her. Yet she soon began to rejoice that she had heard them. They were of sobering

tendency; they allayed agitation; they composed, and conse-
quently must make her happier.

Frederick Wentworth had used such words, or something like
them, but without an idea that they would be carried round to
her. He had thought her wretchedly altered, and, in the first
moment of appeal, had spoken as he felt. He had not forgiven
Anne Elliot. She had used him ill; deserted and disappointed him;
and worse, she had shown a feebleness of character in doing so,
which his own decided, confident temper could not endure. She
had given him up to oblige others. It had been the effect of over-
persuasion. It had been weakness and timidity.

He had been most warmly attached to her, and had never seen
a woman since whom he thought her equal; but, except for some
natural sensation of curiosity, he had no desire of meeting her
again. Her power with him was gone for ever.

JANE AUSTEN

The Mirror

To make a clean sweep was the easiest part,
Though difficult enough. Anger of grief
Strengthened her hand and kept the silly heart
From dallying over his relics for relief.

To burn the letters, send back the keepsakes, wipe
His fingerprints off what little remained her own—
The girl stood over herself with a swift whip
And lashed until the outrageous task was done.

She had detached her flesh from his flesh, torn
It loose like a sea-anemone from a rock.
Now in that bare room where, lest he return,
All else was changed (she could not change the lock)

She took one careful invalid step, gauging
How much the ice of solitude would bear,
Then sat to her glass, as women do, assuaging
Chaotic thoughts with the clear, known image there.

No blood at the lips, no scars on the limpid brow,
Her face gazed out, vacant and undistracted,
A mere proscenium—nothing to show
For the tragedy, or farce, lately enacted.

True, it was not the first time nor the second
That love had lured her into a dead end.
She knew it all: but on this she had not reckoned—
The trick of a mirror upon the wall behind

Which cast in hers an endless, ever-diminished
Sequence of selves rejected and alone,
Cast back in her teeth the falsehood that she was finished
With love's calamities, having survived this one.

Seven devils, each worse than the one she had expelled,
Entering now that swept and garnished room,
Image on image on image in the glass she felt
Sucking her down into a vacuum,

A hell of narrowing circles. Time and again
Would she sit at the glass, helplessly reviling
The self that had linked her failures into a chain,
An ineluctable pattern. Love's too willing

Victim and love's unwilling poisoner, she
Would always kill the joys for which she died.
'Deep within you,' whispered the fiends, 'must be
'A double agent, false to either side. . . .'

Fallen at last, hurled beyond hope or terror,
Gathering doom about her, the girl now saw
Her hand, which had not strength to break the mirror,
Grope for the sleeping tablets in a drawer.

C. DAY LEWIS

‘

The Willow Cabin

*Caroline Seward, a young and extremely gifted actress, meets,
and almost at once falls irrevocably in love with, Michael
Knowle, a successful surgeon who is married and sixteen years
older than she. They become lovers and he also becomes the
centre of her life.*

By then, she thought, the theatre had ceased to be her profession;
her profession was Michael.

'And I didn't do so well at that one, in the beginning.'

She was reluctant to let her memory take over at this point.
The path of these thoughts would lead her into dark places; past
all the betrayal of that first confident assurance that she could love
him forever and be content with his way of loving. She must pass
by vows and recantations, by pain that was as violent as tooth-
ache; past unreasonable jealousy, humble withdrawal and the
sterile suffering that went on throughout his absences. She must
taste again the pure hatred of Mercedes, who was less a target for
jealousy than an ultimate obstacle, the wife who was adamant,
the archpriestess of the Spoilers-of-the-Fun. She must see herself
swayed like a person under a spell; with Michael standing by,
always courteous, patient and truthful; the rock of strength on
which, in her darkest moments, she could feel that she dashed
herself to pieces.

'When did it begin to be all right?' she asked herself bewil-
deredly. 'How? Did I learn to behave, or did he learn to love me
more? Or both?'

Because, lately, she could feel that she had won; that in patient
bondage to the hopeless thing, she had builded better than she
knew; that in contradition to all theories of love, she had tied him

to her by simple devotion. Was that too pretty a translation of the truth, she wondered, staring at the last gleam of red among the coals in the grate. 'Oh, you can make it look any way you like. You could say that you had made yourself necessary to him.' (And if you looked at it in that light, you would see that it was a severe and exact apprenticeship, whose training had left no time for any other.)

Slowly, she had learned to rage in secret and to weep alone. She had learned to hide from him the small worries that he begged to be allowed to share. She had discovered early that she could make him laugh, and it became an obligation always to make him laugh, to save the funny things for him and hand them over, as toys to a child, at the day's end. She had cured herself of questioning him, rebuking him and sulking at him. To suit his time-table, she would cancel at the shortest notice any prior engagement. She had set herself the task of being always decorative, always good-tempered, always punctual; this last was easy, for she was anxious never to lose a second of him; at least he looked grateful when he found her waiting. She had forced upon herself the study of his work, solemnly reading manuals of surgery that sickened her, acquiring medical knowledge from all the sources that she could tap. She had made the decision to stay on at the Rufford Hotel because this was a place where he could come at erratic hours, to sit in the elaborate lounge and eat and drink, still looking respectable and making love only in words. It was when that rendezvous became too public, when the snatched private hours failed to satisfy him, that she began to go regularly to the house in Manchester Square.

Looking back, she could see other assets than the sweetness of his company. From him she had learned wisdom; she respected him even when her mind was at its most detached, seeing them both for what they were. She could sneer at the list of losses on the other side of the balance-sheet . . .

PAMELA FRANKAU

Sonnet XXXIV

Farewell! thou are too dear for my possessing,
  And like enough thou know'st thy estimate:
Thy charter of thy worth gives thee releasing;
  My bonds in thee are all determinate.
For how do I hold thee but by thy granting?
  And for that riches where is my deserving?
The cause of this fair gift in me is wanting,
  And so my patent back again is swerving.
Thyself thou gavest, thy own worth then not knowing,
  Or me, to whom thou gavest it, else mistaking;
So thy great gift, upon misprision growing,
  Comes home again, on better judgement making.
    Thus have I had thee, as a dream doth flatter,
    In sleep a king, but, waking, no such matter.

WILLIAM SHAKESPEARE

Sonnet XV

Since there's no help, come let us kiss and part.
  Nay, I have done; you get no more of me,
And I am glad, yea, glad with all my heart,
  That thus so cleanly I myself can free;
Shake hands for ever, cancel all our vows,
  And when we meet at any time again,
Be it not seen in either of our brows
  That we one jot of former love retain.
Now at the last gasp of Love's latest breath,
  When, his pulse failing, Passion speechless lies,
When Faith is kneeling by his bed of death,
  And Innocence is closing up his eyes,
    Now if thou wouldst, when all have given him over,
    From death to life thou mightst him yet recover.

MICHAEL DRAYTON

Non sum qualis eram bonae sub regno Cynarae

Last night, ah, yesternight, betwixt her lips and mine
There fell thy shadow, Cynara! thy breath was shed
Upon my soul between the kisses and the wine;
And I was desolate and sick of an old passion,
    Yea, I was desolate and bowed my head:
I have been faithful to thee, Cynara! in my fashion.

All night upon mine heart I felt her warm heart beat,
Night-long within mine arms in love and sleep she lay;
Surely the kisses of her bought red mouth were sweet;
But I was desolate and sick of an old passion,
    When I awoke and found the dawn was gray:
I have been faithful to thee, Cynara! in my fashion.

I have forgot much, Cynara! gone with the wind,
Flung roses, roses riotously with the throng,
Dancing, to put thy pale, lost lilies out of mind;
But I was desolate and sick of an old passion,
    Yea, all the time, because the dance was long:
I have been faithful to thee, Cynara! in my fashion.

I cried for madder music and for stronger wine,
But when the feast is finished and the lamps expire,
Then falls thy shadow, Cynara! the night is thine;
And I am desolate and sick of an old passion,
    Yea, hungry for the lips of my desire:
I have been faithful to thee, Cynara! in my fashion.

ERNEST DOWSON

Twelfth Night (Act II, Sc. iv)

Here is Viola again, covertly expressing her love for the Duke.

DUKE: Once more, Cesario,
Get thee to yond sovereign cruelty:
Tell her, my love, more noble than the world,
Prizes not quantity of dirty lands;
The parts that fortune hath bestow'd upon her,
Tell her, I hold as giddily as fortune;
But 'tis that miracle and queen of gems
That nature pranks her in attracts my soul.

VIOLA: But if she cannot love you, sir?

DUKE: I cannot be so answer'd.

VIOLA: Sooth, but you must.
Say that some lady, as perhaps there is,
Hath for your love as great a pang of heart
As you have for Olivia: you cannot love her;
You tell her so; must she not then be answer'd?

DUKE: There is no woman's sides
Can bide the beating of so strong a passion
As love doth give my heart; no woman's heart
So big, to hold so much; they lack retention.
Alas, their love may be call'd appetite,—
No motion of the liver, but the palate,—
That suffer surfeit, cloyment and revolt;
But mine is all as hungry as the sea,
And can digest as much: make no compare
Between that love a woman can bear me
And that I owe Olivia.

VIOLA: Ay, but I know,—

DUKE: What dost thou know?

VIOLA: Too well what love women to men may owe:
In faith, they are as true of heart as we.
My father had a daughter loved a man,
As it might be, perhaps, were I a woman,
I should your lordship.

DUKE: And what's her history?

VIOLA: A blank, my lord. She never told her love,
But let concealment, like a worm i' the bud,
Feed on her damask cheek: she pined in thought
And with a green and yellow melancholy
She sat like patience on a monument,
Smiling at grief. Was not this love indeed?
We men may say more, swear more: but indeed
Our shows are more than will; for still we prove
Much in our vows, but little in our love.

WILLIAM SHAKESPEARE

Sonnet
(from Amoretti)

Lacking my love, I go from place to place
Like a young fawn that late hath lost the hind;
And seek each where, where last I saw her face
Whose image yet I carry fresh in mind.
I seek the fields with her late footing signed,
I seek her bower with her late presence decked,
Yet nor in field nor bower I can her find;
Yet field and bower are full of her aspéct:
But, when mine eyes I thereunto direct,
They idly back return to me again,
And, when I hope to see their true objéct,
I find myself but fed with fancies vain.
Cease then, mine eyes, to seek her self to see;
And let my thoughts behold her self in me.

EDMUND SPENSER

Sleep On
(from The Exequy)

Sleep on, my love, in thy cold bed
Never to be disquieted!
My last good night! Thou wilt not wake
Till I thy fate shall overtake;
Till age, or grief, or sickness must
Marry my body to that dust
It so much loves, and fill the room
My heart keeps empty in thy tomb.
Stay for me there; I will not fail
To meet thee in that hollow vale;
And think not much of my delay;
I am already on the way,
And follow thee with all the speed
Desire can make, or sorrows breed.

HENRY KING

John Keats to Fanny Brawne

[5 July 1820]
Wednesday Morng.

My dearest Girl,
 I have been a walk this morning with a book in my hand, but as usual I have been occupied with nothing but you I wish I could say in an agreeable manner. I am tormented day and night. They talk of my going to Italy. 'Tis certain I shall never recover if I am to be so long separate from you yet with all this devotion to you I cannot persuade myself into any confidence of you. Past experience connected with the fact of my long separation from you gives me agonies which are scarcely to be talked of. When your mother comes I shall be very sudden and expert in asking her whether you have been to Mrs Dilke's, for she might say no to make me easy. I am literally worn to death, which seems my only recourse. I cannot

forget what has pass'd. What? nothing with a man of the world, but to me deathful. I will get rid of this as much as possible. When you were in the habit of flirting with Brown you would have left off, could your own heart have felt one half of one pang mine did. Brown is a good sort of Man—he did not know he was doing me to death by inches. I feel the effect of every one of those hours in my side now; and for that cause, though he has done me many services, though I know his love and friendship for me, though at this moment I should be without pence were it not for his assistance, I will never see or speak to him until we are both old men, if we are to be. I *will* resent my heart having been made a football. You will call this madness. I have heard you say that it was not unpleasant to wait a few years—you have amusements—your mind is away—you have not brooded over one idea as I have, and how should you? You are to me an object intensely desireable— the air I breathe in a room empty of you is unhealthy. I am not the same to you—no—you can wait—you have a thousand activities—you can be happy without me. Any party, any thing to fill up the day has been enough. How have you pass'd this month? Who have you smil'd with? All this may seem savage in me. You do not feel as I do—you do not know what it is to love—one day you may—your time is not come. Ask yourself how many unhappy hours Keats has caused you in Loneliness. For myself I have been a Martyr the whole time, and for this reason I speak; the confession is forc'd from me by the torture. I appeal to you by the blood of that Christ you believe in: Do not write to me if you have done anything this month which it would have pained me to have seen. You may have altered—if you have not—if you still behave in dancing rooms and other societies as I have seen you—I do not want to live—if you have done so I wish this coming night may be my last. I cannot live without you, and not only you but *chaste you; virtuous you.* The Sun rises and sets, the day passes, and you follow the bent of your inclination to a certain extent— you have no conception of the quantity of miserable feeling that passes through me in a day.—Be serious! Love is not a plaything— and again do not write unless you can do it with a crystal conscience. I would sooner die for want of you than—

Yours for ever

J. Keats

From Don Juan

'They tell me 'tis decided you depart:
   'Tis wise—'tis well, but not the less a pain;
I have no further claim on your young heart,
   Mine is the victim, and would be again:
To love too much has been the only art
   I used;—I write in haste, and if a stain
Be on this sheet, 'tis not what it appears;
My eyeballs burn and throb, but have no tears.

'I loved, I love you, for this love have lost
   State, station, heaven, mankind's, my own esteem,
And yet cannot regret what it hath cost,
   So dear is still the memory of that dream;
Yet, if I name my guilt, 'tis not to boast,
   None can deem harshlier of me than I deem:
I trace this scrawl because I cannot rest—
I've nothing to reproach or to request.

'Man's love is of man's life a thing apart,
   'Tis woman's whole existence; man may range
The court, camp, church, the vessel, and the mart;
   Sword, gown, gain, glory, offer in exchange
Pride, fame, ambition, to fill up his heart,
   And few there are whom these cannot estrange;
Men have all these resources, we but one,
To love again, and be again undone.

'You will proceed in pleasure, and in pride,
   Beloved and loving many; all is o'er
For me on earth, except some years to hide
   My shame and sorrow deep in my heart's core:
These I could bear, but cannot cast aside
   The passion which still rages as before,—
And so farewell—forgive me, love me—No,
That word is idle now—but let it go.

'My breast has been all weakness, is so yet;
   But still I think I can collect my mind;
My blood still rushes where my spirit's set,
   As roll the waves before the settled wind;
My heart is feminine, nor can forget—
   To all, except one image, madly blind;
So shakes the needle, and so stands the pole,
As vibrates my fond heart to my fix'd soul.

'I have no more to say, but linger still,
   And dare not set my seal upon this sheet,
And yet I may as well the task fulfil,
   My misery can scarce be more complete:
I had not lived till now, could sorrow kill;
   Death shuns the wretch who fain the blow would meet,
And I must even survive this last adieu,
And bear with life to love and pray for you!'

This note was written upon gilt-edged paper
   With a neat little crow-quill, slight and new;
Her small white hand could hardly reach the taper,
   It trembled as magnetic needles do,
And yet she did not let one tear escape her;
   The seal a sun-flower; '*Elle vous suit partout,*'
The motto, cut upon a white cornelian;
The wax was superfine, its hue vermilion.

LORD BYRON

Mrs Penruddock's Last Letter to Her Husband

*Mr Penruddock, when he received his wife's note, was under
sentence of death by Cromwell for his share in the Royalist
rising at Exeter, and was beheaded there in 1655.*

May 3, 1655.

My dear heart,—My sad parting was so far from making me
forget you, that I scarce thought upon myself since, but wholly

upon you. Those dear embraces which I yet feel, and shall never lose, being the faithful testimonies of an indulgent husband, have charmed my soul to such a reverence of your remembrance, that were it possible, I would, with my own blood, cement your dead limbs to live again, and (with reverence) think it no sin to rob heaven a little longer of a martyr. Oh my dear, you must now pardon my passion, this being my last (oh, fatal word!) that ever you will receive from me; and know, that until the last minute that I can imagine you shall live, I shall sacrifice the prayers of a Christian, and the groans of an afflicted wife. And when you are not (which sure by sympathy I shall know), I shall wish my own dissolution with you, that so we may go hand in hand to heaven. 'Tis too late to tell you what I have, or rather have not done for you; how being turned out of doors because I came to beg mercy; the Lord lay not your blood to their charge.

I would fain discourse longer with you, but dare not; passion begins to drown my reason, and will rob me of my devoirs, which is all I have left to serve you. Adieu, therefore, ten thousand times, my dearest dear; and since I must never see you more, take this prayer,—May your faith be so strengthened that your constancy may continue; and then I know heaven will receive you; whither grief and love will in a short time (I hope) translate,

My dear,

Your sad, but constant wife, even to love your ashes when dead,

ARUNDEL PENRUDDOCK.

May the 3d, 1655, eleven o'clock at night. Your children beg your blessing, and present their duties to you.

Mr Penruddock's Last Letter to His Wife

May 1655.

Dearest, best of Creatures!—I had taken leave of the world when I received yours: it did at once recall my fondness to life, and enable me to resign it. As I am sure I shall leave none behind me like you, which weakens my resolution to part from you, so when I reflect I am going to a place where there are none but such as you, I recover my courage. But fondness breaks in upon me; and as I would not have my tears flow to-morrow, when your husband, and the father of our dear babes, is a public spectacle, do not think meanly of me, that I give way to grief now in private, when I see my sand run so fast, and within a few hours I am to leave you helpless, and exposed to the merciless and insolent that have wrongfully put me to a shameless death, and will object the shame to my poor children. I thank you for all your goodness to me, and will endeavour so to die as to do nothing unworthy that virtue in which we have mutually supported each other, and for which I desire you not to repine that I am first to be rewarded, since you ever preferred me to yourself in all other things. Afford me, with cheerfulness, the precedence of this: I desire your prayers in the article of death; for my own will then be offered for you and yours.

J. PENRUDDOCK.

Letter from Emma Hamilton About Nelson

. . . I am anxious and agitated to see Him. I never shall be well till I do see him, the disappointment would kill me. I love him, I adore him, my mind and soul is now transported with the thoughts of that Blessed Extatic moment when I shall see Him embrace Him. My love is no common love. It may be a sin to love, I say it might have been a sin when I was another's but I had then more merit in trying to suppress it. I am *now Free* and I must sin on and love Him more than ever, it is a crime worth going to Hell for. For should I not be an ungrateful unfeeling wretch not to pay two fold with love the man that so idolises me, that adores me. May God only spare Him and send Him safe back. I shall be at Merton till I see Him as He *particularly* wishes our first meeting should be there . . .

Dear Alf

Anonymous letter from a newspaper. The writer died a few days after it was written.

Dear Alf,
    I seen you last night in my dream. O my dear I cried at waking up. What a silly girl you been and got. The pain is bad this morning but I laugh at the sollum cloks of the sisters and the sawbones.

I can see they think I am booked but they don't know what has befalen between you and me. How could I die and leave my Dear. I spill my medecin this morning thinking of my Dear. Hopeing this finds you well no more now from yours truly Liz.

Antony and Cleopatra (Act I, Sc v)

Here is the scene when Antony has left Cleopatra to return to Rome.

CLEOPATRA: O Charmian,
            Where think'st thou he is now? Stands he, or
                sits he?
            Or does he walk? or is he on his horse?
            O happy horse, to bear the weight of Antony!
            Do bravely, horse! for wot'st thou whom
                thou movest?
            The demi-Atlas of this earth, the arm
            And burgonet of men. He's speaking now,
            Or murmuring, 'Where's my serpent of old
                Nile?'
            For so he calls me: now I feed myself
            With most delicious poison. Think on me,
            That am with Phoebus' amorous pinches black
            And wrinkled deep in time? Broad-fronted
                Caesar,
            When thou wast here above the ground, I was
            A morsel for a monarch: and great Pompey
            Would stand and make his eyes grow in my
                brow;
            There would he anchor his aspect and die
            With looking on his life.
                                    Enter ALEXAS
ALEXAS: Sovereign of Egypt, hail!
CLEOPATRA: How much unlike art thou Mark Antony!
            Yet, coming from him, that great medicine
                hath
            With his tinct gilded thee.
            How goes it with my brave Mark Antony?

ALEXAS: Last thing he did, dear queen,
He kiss'd—the last of many doubled kisses—
This orient pearl. His speech sticks in my
heart.

CLEOPATRA: Mine ear must pluck it thence.

ALEXAS: 'Good friend,' quoth he,
'Say, the firm Roman to great Egypt sends
This treasure of an oyster; at whose foot,
To mend the petty present, I will piece
Her opulent throne with kingdoms; all the east,
Say thou, shall call her mistress.' So he nodded,
And soberly did mount an arm-gaunt steed,
Who neigh'd so high, that what I would have
spoke
Was beastly dumb'd by him.

. . . .

WILLIAM SHAKESPEARE

Going to the Warres

Tell me not (Sweet) I am unkinde,
    That from the Nunnerie
Of thy chaste breast, and quiet minde,
    To Warre and Armes I flie.

True; a new Mistresse now I chase,
    The first Foe in the Field;
And with a stronger Faith imbrace
    A Sword, a Horse, a Shield.

Yet this Inconstancy is such,
    As you too shall adore;
I could not love thee (Deare) so much,
    Lov'd I not Honour more.

RICHARD LOVELACE

Remember

Remember me when I am gone away,
　Gone far away into the silent land;
　When you can no more hold me by the hand,
Nor I half turn to go yet turning stay.
Remember me when no more day by day
　You tell me of our future that you planned:
　Only remember me; you understand
It will be late to counsel then or pray.
Yet if you should forget me for a while
　And afterwards remember, do not grieve:
　For if the darkness and corruption leave
A vestige of the thoughts that once I had,
Better by far you should forget and smile
　Than that you should remember and be sad.

CHRISTINA ROSSETTI

Antony and Cleopatra (Act IV, Sc xiv)

*Antony, returned to Egypt and thinking that Cleopatra has
betrayed him, quarrels with her, whereupon she sends word
that she has died from grief. Antony falls upon his sword,
which mortally wounds him, but he does not die at once.
Here is the last scene between the lovers.*

　　　　　Enter above, CLEOPATRA, CHARMIAN, *and* IRAS
CLEOPATRA: O Charmian, I will never go from hence.
CHARMIAN: Be comforted, dear madam.
CLEOPATRA: 　　　　　　　　No, I will not.
　　　All strange and terrible events are welcome,
　　　But comforts we despise; our size of sorrow,
　　　Proportion'd to our cause, must be as great
　　　As that which makes it.

Enter DIOMEDES, *below*

                              How now! is he dead?

DIOMEDES: His death's upon him but not dead.
Look out o' the other side your monument;
His guard have brought him thither.

Enter, below, ANTONY, *borne by the* Guard

CLEOPATRA: O sun,
Burn the great sphere thou movest in!
   darkling stand
The varying shore o'the world! O Antony,
Antony, Antony! Help, Charmian, help, Iras,
   help;
Help, friends below; let's draw him hither.

ANTONY: Peace:
Not Caesar's valour hath o'erthrown Antony,
But Antony's hath triumph'd on itself.

CLEOPATRA: So it should be, that none but Antony
Should conquer Antony; but woe't is so!

ANTONY: I am dying, Egypt, dying; only
I here importune death awhile, until
Of many thousand kisses the poor last
I lay upon thy lips.

CLEOPATRA: I dare not, dear,
Dear my lord, pardon, I dare not,
Lest I be taken: not the imperious show
Of the full-fortuned Caesar ever shall
Be brooch'd with me; if knife, drugs, serpents,
   have
Edge, sting, or operation, I am safe:
Your wife Octavia, with her modest eyes
And still conclusion, shall acquire no honour
Demuring upon me. But come, come,
   Antony,—
Help me, my women,—we must draw thee up;
Assist, good friends.

ANTONY: O quick, or I am gone.

CLEOPATRA: Here's sport indeed! How heavy weighs my
   lord!

Our strength is all gone into heaviness;
That makes the weight. Had I great Juno's
    power,
The strong-wing'd Mercury should fetch thee
    up
And set thee by Jove's side. Yet come a
    little,—
Wishers were ever fools:—O, come, come,
    come;

               [They draw Antony up]
And welcome, welcome! die where thou hast
    lived:
Quicken with kissing, had my lips that power,
Thus would I wear them out.

ALL: A heavy sight!

ANTONY: I am dying, Egypt, dying:
Give me some wine, and let me speak a little.

CLEOPATRA: No, let me speak, and let me rail so high,
That the false housewife Fortune break her
    wheel,
Provoked by my offence.

ANTONY: One word, sweet queen:
Of Caesar seek your honour, with your safety.
    —O!

CLEOPATRA: They do not go together.

ANTONY: Gentle, hear me:
None about Caesar trust but Proculeius.

CLEOPATRA: My resolution and my hands I'll trust;
None about Caesar.

ANTONY: The miserable change now at my end
Lament nor sorrow at, but please your
    thoughts
In feeding them with those my former fortunes
Wherein I lived, the greatest prince o' the
    world,
The noblest; and do now not basely die,
Nor cowardly put off my helmet to
My countryman, a Roman by a Roman

	Valiantly vanquish'd. Now my spirit is going;
	I can no more.
CLEOPATRA:	Noblest of men, woo't die?

Valiantly vanquish'd. Now my spirit is going;
I can no more.

CLEOPATRA: Noblest of men, woo't die?
Hast thou no care of me? shall I abide
In this dull world, which in thy absence is
No better than a sty?—O, see, my women,
The crown o'the earth doth melt. My lord!
                         [*Antony dies*]
O, wither'd is the garland of the war,
The soldier's pole is fall'n: young boys and
    girls
Are level now with men; the odds is gone,
And there is nothing left remarkable
Beneath the visiting moon.   [*She faints*]

CHARMIAN: O, quietness, lady.
IRAS: She's dead too, our sovereign.
CHARMIAN: Lady!
IRAS: Madam!
CHARMIAN: O madam, madam, madam!
IRAS: Royal Egypt, Empress!
CHARMIAN: Peace, peace, Iras!
CLEOPATRA: No more, but e'en a woman, and commanded
By such poor passion as the maid that milks
And does the meanest chares. It were for me
To throw my sceptre at the injurious gods,
To tell them that this world did equal theirs
Till they had stol'n our jewel. All's but naught;
Patience is sottish, and impatience does
Become a dog that's mad: then is it sin
To rush into the secret house of death,
Ere death dare come to us? How do you,
    women?
What, what! good cheer! Why, how now,
    Charmian!
My noble girls! Ah, women, women, look,
Our lamp is spent, it's out! Good sirs, take
    heart:

We'll bury him; and then, what's brave, what's
  noble,
Let's do it after the high Roman fashion,
And make death proud to take us. Come,
  away:
This case of that huge spirit now is cold.
Ah, women, women! Come; we have no
  friend
But resolution, and the briefest end.
[*Exeunt; those above bearing off Antony's body*]

WILLIAM SHAKESPEARE

Renouncement

I must not think of thee; and, tired yet strong,
  I shun the thought that lurks in all delight—
  The thought of thee—and in the blue Heaven's height,
And in the dearest passage of a song.

Oh, just beyond the fairest thoughts that throng
  This breast, the thought of thee waits hidden, yet bright;
  But it must never, never come in sight;
I must stop short of thee the whole day long.

But when sleep comes to close each difficult day,
  When night gives pause to the long watch I keep,
    And all my bonds I needs must loose apart,
Must doff my will as raiment laid away,—
  With the first dream that comes with the first sleep
    I run, I run, I am gathered to thy heart.

ALICE MEYNELL

Waly, Waly (Scottish Ballad)

O, waly, waly up the bank,
And waly, waly doun the brae,
And waly, waly yon burnside
Where I and my love wont tae gae.

I set my back against an aik,
I thocht it was a trusty tree,
But first it bent and syne it brak
And sae did my love lichtlie me.

O, waly, waly, gin love be bonny,
A little time when it is new;
But when 'tis auld it waxeth cauld
And fades away like morning dew.

O, had I wist before I kissed
That love had been sae ill tae win,
I'd locked my heart in a golden kyst
And pinned it wi' a siller pin.

O wherefore should I busk my heid,
Or wherefore should I came my hair?
For my true love has me forsook,
And says he'll never love me mair.

When we cam intae Glasgow toun,
We were a comely sicht tae see;
My love was clad in the black velvet,
And I mysel' in cramoisie.

And O that my dear babe were born,
And set upon its nurse's knee,
And I mysel' were dead and gone,
And the green grass growing over me.

Victoria

Johannes, the miller's son, has always loved the daughter of the manor which is like a small castle. When they were children, he was sometimes allowed to help the castle children and their friends in their amusements. They grow up, and Victoria becomes engaged to a rich lieutenant. Johannes makes his name as a writer. Just before the marriage the lieutenant is killed in a shooting accident. Victoria comes to Johannes and tells him that it is he she has always loved: her parents made her engage herself to a rich man to pay the family debts. Johannes has to tell her that he has become engaged. But that affair also comes to an end; he hears that Victoria is ill: that she has been declining ever since her fiancé died. Then he gets a letter, and the news that Victoria is dead. Here is her letter.

Johannes remained standing with the letter in his hand. Victoria was dead. Again and again he spoke her name—in a voice devoid of emotion, almost callous. He looked down at the letter and recognized the writing; there were capital letters and small letters, the lines were straight, and she who had written them was dead!

Then he made his way past the door and up the stairs, found the right key and let himself in. His room was cold and dark. He drew a chair to the window and by the last remaining light of day he read Victoria's letter.

Dear Johannes!

When you read this letter I shall be dead. Everything seems so strange now; I don't feel ashamed to write to you any more and I'm writing just as if nothing had ever happened to prevent it. Before, when I was still fully alive, I would rather have suffered night and day than written to you again; but now I have started to die and I don't think in that way any longer. Strangers have seen me bleed, the doctor has examined me and says I've only got a tiny bit of one lung left, so why should I feel embarrassed any more?

I have been lying here in bed thinking about the last words I spoke to you. It was in the wood that evening. I never thought then that they would be my last words, or I would have said goodbye then and there and thanked you. Now I shall never see you again, so I'm sorry now that I didn't throw myself at your feet and kiss your shoes and the ground you trod on, to show you how far beyond words I loved you. I have been lying here yesterday and today wishing I was well enough to get away and go home again and walk in the wood and find the place where we sat when you held both my hands; because then I could lie there and see if I couldn't find some trace of you and kiss all the heather around. But now I can't come home unless perhaps I get a little bit better, as Mamma thinks I will.

Dear Johannes, it is strange to think that all I've ever managed to do was to come into the world and love you and now say goodbye to life. Imagine how strange it is to lie here and wait for the day and the hour. I am departing step by step from life and the people in the street and the rumbling of carriages; I don't suppose I shall ever see the spring again, and these houses and streets and trees in the park will still be here when I am gone. Today I managed to sit up in bed and ook out the window for a little. Down by the corner I saw two people meet; they raised their hats and shook hands and laughed at what they said; but it was so strange to think that I who was lying watching them was going to die. I began thinking: those two down there don't know that I'm lying here waiting for my time; but even if they knew they would shake hands and talk to each other just the same. Last night when it was dark I thought my last hour had come, my heart stopped beating, and in the distance I seemed already to hear eternity rushing towards me. But the next moment I was back from my long journey and began breathing again. I can't begin to describe the feeling. But Mamma thinks it may only have been the river and the waterfall at home that I was hearing.

Dear God—if you only knew how much I have loved you, Johannes. I have never managed to show you, there have been so many obstacles, above all my own nature. Papa too was his own worst enemy, and I am his daughter. But now that I am about to die and it is all too late I am writing to you once again to tell you. I ask myself why I am doing so when it means little to you in any case, especially now that I am about to die; but I want so much to be near you at the end, so that at least I don't feel any lonelier than before. When you read this letter it will be as if I can see your shoulders and hands and see every movement you make as you hold the letter in front of you and read it. Then we won't be so far apart, I think to myself. I can't send for you, I haven't the right. Mamma wanted to send for you two days ago, but I'd rather write. And I'd like it best if you remembered me as I was once, before I became ill. I remember you . . . [here she had skipped a few words] . . . my eyes and eyebrows; but they are no longer the same. That is another reason I didn't want you to come. And also I want to ask you not to come and look at me in the coffin. I suppose I shall look much the same as when I was alive, only slightly paler, and I shall be in my yellow dress; but all the same, you would regret it if you came and saw me.

I've been writing this letter at intervals all day, and still I haven't managed to tell you a thousandth part of what I wanted to say. It's so terrible for me to have to die, I don't want to, I still pray to God in my heart that perhaps I may get a bit better, even if only until the spring. Then the days are light and there are leaves on the trees. If I got well again now I would never be horrid to you again, Johannes. How I've wept and thought about it! Oh God, I would go out and touch all the cobblestones and stop and thank every single step of the stairs as I passed, and be kind to everyone. It wouldn't matter how much I suffered if only I was allowed to live. I would never complain about anything again, no, I'd smile at anyone who attacked me and hit me, and thank and praise God if only I might live. My life is so unlived, I've never done anything to help anybody, and now this wasted life is going to end. If you knew how unwilling I am to die, perhaps you would do something, do everything in your power. I know you can't do much, of course; but I thought that if you and everyone else prayed for me and refused to let me go, then God would grant me life. Ah, how grateful I would be then, and I would never be unkind to anyone again, but would smile at my lot, whatever it was, if only I was allowed to live.

Mamma is sitting here weeping. She sat here all night as well and wept for me. This helps me a little, it softens the bitterness of my leaving. And today I thought: what would you do if I came up to you in the street one day in my best clothes and didn't say anything to wound you any more but gave you a rose which I had bought beforehand? But then the next moment I remembered that I can never do the things I want any more; because I know that I'm never going to get well again before I die. I weep so much, I lie still and weep ceaselessly and inconsolably; it doesn't hurt my chest except when I sob aloud. Johannes, my dear, dear friend, the only one I have loved on this earth, come to me now and be here for a little while when it begins to grow dark. I shan't weep then, but smile as well as I can, from sheer joy at your coming.

No, where are my pride and my courage! I am not my father's daughter now; but that's because my strength has left me. I have suffered for a long time now, Johannes, since long before these last days. I suffered when you were abroad, and later, ever since I came to town in the spring, I have done nothing but suffer every day. I never knew before how endlessly long the night could be. I've seen you twice in the street; once you were humming as you passed me, but you didn't see me. I'd hoped to see you at the Seiers'; but you never came. I wouldn't have spoken to you or approached you, but would have been thankful just to see you in the distance. But you never came. And then I thought that perhaps it was on my account that you never came. At eleven o'clock I began dancing, because I couldn't bear to wait any longer. Yes, Johannes, I've loved you, loved only you all my life. It's Victoria who is writing this, and God is reading it over my shoulder.

And now I must bid you farewell, it's almost dark now and I can't see any longer. Goodbye, Johannes, and thank you for every day. When I fly away from the earth I shall go on thanking you right to the end and saying your name to myself all the way. May you be happy, then, all your life, and forgive me for the wrong I've done you and for never having thrown myself at your feet and asked your forgiveness. I do so now with all my heart. Be happy, Johannes; and goodbye for ever. And thank you once again for every single day and hour. I can't manage any more.

Yours,
Victoria

Now I've had the lamp lit and have got much more light. I have lain in a trance and again been far from the earth. Thank God, I didn't find it so unpleasant this time, I could even hear some music, and above all it wasn't dark. I am so thankful. But now I have no more strength left to write. Goodbye, my beloved . . .

KNUT HAMSUN

The Sharp Ridge

Since now I dare not ask
Any gift from you, or gentle task,
Or lover's promise—nor yet refuse
Whatever I can give and you dare choose—
Have pity on us both: choose well
On this sharp ridge dividing death from hell.

ROBERT GRAVES

Remembrance

Cold in the earth—and the deep snow piled above thee,
   Far, far removed, cold in the dreary grave!
Have I forgot, my only Love, to love thee,
   Severed at last by Time's all-severing wave?

Now, when alone, do my thoughts no longer hover
   Over the mountains, on that northern shore,
Resting their wings where heath and fern-leaves cover
   Thy noble heart for ever, ever more?

Cold in the earth—and fifteen wild Decembers
   From those brown hills have melted into spring:
Faithful, indeed, is the spirit that remembers
   After such years of change and suffering!

Sweet Love of youth, forgive, if I forget thee,
   While the world's tide is bearing me along;
Other desires and other hopes beset me,
   Hopes which obscure, but cannot do thee wrong!

No later light has lightened up my heaven,
  No second morn has ever shone for me;
All my life's bliss from thy dear life was given,
  All my life's bliss is in the grave with thee.

But, when the days of golden dreams had perished,
  And even Despair was powerless to destroy,
Then did I learn how existence could be cherished,
  Strengthened and fed, without the aid of joy.

Then did I check the tears of useless passion—
  Weaned my young soul from yearning after thine;
Sternly denied its burning wish to hasten
  Down to that tomb already more than mine.

And, even yet, I dare not let it languish,
  Dare not indulge in memory's rapturous pain;
Once drinking deep of that divinest anguish,
  How could I seek the empty world again?

EMILY BRONTË

The Pursuit of Love

These two passages are at the end of the novel, when Linda, who is pregnant and, with her lover, Fabrice, fighting with the French Underground, gets her one and only letter.

In point of fact Linda never got any letters at all. She had not seen her English friends now for so long, they were scattered in the war to the ends of the earth, and, though they might not have forgotten about Linda, she was no longer in their lives. But, of course, there was only one thing she wanted, a letter, a line even, from Fabrice. Just after Christmas it came. It was forwarded in a typewritten envelope from Carlton Gardens with General de Gaulle's stamp on it. Linda, when she saw it lying on the hall table, became perfectly white. She seized it and rushed up to her bedroom.
  About an hour later she came to find me.
  'Oh, darling,' she said, her eyes full of tears. 'I've been all this

time and I can't read one word. Isn't it torture? Could you have a look?'

She gave me a sheet of the thinnest paper I ever saw, on which were scratched, apparently with a rusty pin, a series of perfectly incomprehensible hieroglyphics. I could not make out one single word either, it seemed to bear no relation to handwriting, the marks in no way resembled letters.

'What can I do?' said poor Linda. 'Oh, Fanny.'

'Let's ask Davey,' I said.

She hesitated a little over this, but feeling that it would be better, however intimate the message, to share it with Davy than not to have it at all, she finally agreed.

Davey said she was quite right to ask him.

'I am very good at French handwriting.'

'Only you wouldn't laugh at it?' Linda said, in a breathless voice like a child.

'No, Linda, I don't regard it as a laughing matter any longer,' Davey replied, looking with love and anxiety at her face, which had become very drawn of late. But when he had studied the paper for some time, he too was obliged to confess himself absolutely stumped by it.

'I've seen a lot of difficult French writings in my life,' he said, 'and this beats them all.'

In the end Linda had to give up. She went about with the piece of paper, like a talisman, in her pocket, but never knew what Fabrice had written to her on it. It was cruelly tantalizing. She wrote to him at Carlton Gardens, but this letter came back with a note regretting that it could not be forwarded.

'Never mind,' she said. 'One day the telephone bell will ring again and he'll be there.'

On the 28th May both our babies were born—both boys. The doctors who said that Linda ought never to have another child were not such idiots after all. It killed her. She died, I think, completely happy, and without having suffered very much, but for us at Alconleigh, for her father and mother, brothers and sisters, for Davey and for Lord Merlin a light went out, a great deal of joy that never could be replaced.

At about the same time as Linda's death Fabrice was caught by the Gestapo and subsequently shot. He was a hero of the Resistance, and his name has become a legend in France.

I have adopted the little Fabrice, with the consent of Christian, his legal father. He has black eyes, the same shape as Linda's blue ones, and is a most beautiful and enchanting child. I love him quite as much as, and perhaps more than, I do my own.

The Bolter came to see me while I was still in the Oxford nursing home where my baby had been born and where Linda had died.

'Poor Linda,' she said, with feeling, 'poor little thing. But Fanny, don't you think perhaps it's just as well? The lives of women like Linda and me are not so much fun when one begins to grow older.'

I didn't want to hurt my mother's feelings by protesting that Linda was not that sort of woman.

'But I think she would have been happy with Fabrice,' I said. 'He was the great love of her life, you know.'

'Oh, dulling,' said my mother, sadly. 'One always thinks that. Every, every time.'

NANCY MITFORD

Modern Love

Thus piteously Love closed what he begat:
The union of this ever-diverse pair!
These two were rapid falcons in a snare,
Condemned to do the flitting of the bat.
Lovers beneath the singing sky of May,
They wandered once; clear as the dew on flowers:
But they fed not on the advancing hours:
Their hearts held cravings for the buried day.
Then each applied to each that fatal knife,
Deep questioning, which probes to endless dole.
Ah, what a dusty answer gets the soul
When hot for certainties in this our life!—
In tragic hints here see what evermore
Moves dark as yonder midnight ocean's force,
Thundering like ramping hosts of warrior horse,
To throw that faint thin line upon the shore!

GEORGE MEREDITH

Napoleon Bonaparte to Josephine Bonaparte (1796)

To citizen Bonaparte,
care of citizen Beauharnais,
6, rue Chantereine,
Paris.

Nice, 10 Germinal, year IV

I have not spent a day without loving you; I have not spent a night without embracing you; I have not so much as drunk a single cup of tea without cursing the pride and ambition which force me to remain separated from the moving spirit of my life. In the midst of my duties, whether I am at the head of my army or inspecting the camps, my beloved Josephine stands alone in my heart, occupies my minds, fills my thoughts. If I am moving away from you with the speed of the Rhône torrent, it is only that I may see you again more quickly. If I rise to work in the middle of the night, it is because this may hasten by a matter of days the arrival of my sweet love. Yet in your letter of the 23rd. and 26th. Ventôse, you call me *vous*. *Vous* yourself! Ah! wretch, how could you have written this letter? How cold it is! And then there are those four days between the 23rd. and the 26th.; what were you doing that you failed to write to your husband? . . . Ah, my love, that *vous*, those four days make me long for my former indifference. Woe to the person responsible! May he, as punishment and penalty, experience what my convictions and the evidence (which is in your friend's favour) would make me experience! Hell has no torments great enough! Nor do the Furies have serpents enough! *Vous! Vous!* Ah! how will things stand in two weeks? . . . My spirit is heavy; my heart is fettered and I am terrified by my fantasies. . . . You love me less; but you will get over the loss. One day you will love me no longer; at least tell me; then I shall know how I have come to deserve this misfortune. . . . Farewell, my wife: the torment, joy, hope and moving spirit of my life; whom I love, whom I fear, who fills me with tender feelings which draw me close to Nature, and with violent impulses as tumultuous as thunder. I ask of you neither eternal love, nor fidelity, but simply . . . *truth*, unlimited honesty. The day when you say 'I love you less', will mark the end of my love and the last day of my life. If my heart were base enough to love without being loved in return I would tear it to pieces. Josephine! Josephine! Remember what I have sometimes said to you: Nature has endowed me with a virile and decisive character. It has built yours out of lace and gossamer. Have you ceased to love me? Forgive me, love of my life, my soul is racked by conflicting forces.

My heart, obsessed by you, is full of fears which prostrate me with misery. . . . I am distressed not to be calling you by name. I shall wait for you to write it.

Farewell! Ah! if you love me less you can never have loved me. In that case I shall truly be pitiable.

Bonaparte

P.S.—The war this year has changed beyond recognition. I have had meat, bread and fodder distributed; my armed cavalry will soon be on the march. My soldiers are showing inexpressible confidence in me; you alone are a source of chagrin to me; you alone are the joy and torment of my life. I send a kiss to your children, whom you do not mention. By God! If you did, your letters would be half as long again. Then visitors at ten o'clock in the morning would not have the pleasure of seeing you. Woman!!!

Epitaph

Colmworth church in Bedfordshire contains a lovely monument erected in 1641 by Lady Catherine to her husband, Sir William Dyer.

My dearest dust, could not thy hasty day
Afford thy drowszy patience leave to stay
One hower longer: so that we might either
Sate up, or gone to bedd together?
But since thy finisht labour hath possest
Thy weary limbs with early rest,
Enjoy it sweetly: and thy widdowe bride
Shall soone repose her by thy slumbring side.
Whose business, now, is only to prepare
My nightly dress, and call to prayre:
Mine eyes wax heavy and ye day growes old.
The dew falls thick, my belovd growes cold.
Draw, draw ye closed curtaynes: and make roome:
My dear, my dearest dust; I come, I come.

Liber Amoris

William Hazlitt's first marriage was a failure: from the end of 1819 he had lived apart from his wife, and in 1820 he went to lodge in London where he fell desperately in love with his landlord's daughter, Sarah Walker, an enigmatic girl of about twenty, trained not to offend men, but adept at keeping them at arm's length. Nobody, it seems, was ever sure what she felt for them—equivocally gentle, very much aware of her own attractions, she was mistress of the art of eluding passion. While Hazlitt was still legally married, she seemed not to discourage his suit, but when he was free she rejected him, and for months he suffered the dual agonies of the idealist who was also a passionate man. The following letter is from his famous Liber Amoris.

My dear P—

You have been very kind to me in this business; but I fear even your indulgence for my infirmities is beginning to fail. To what a state am I reduced, and for what? For fancying a little artful vixen to be an angel and a saint, because she affected to look like one, to hide her rank thoughts and deadly purposes. Has she not murdered me under the mask of the tenderest friendship? And why? Because I have loved her with unutterable love, and sought to make her my wife. You say it is my own 'outrageous conduct' that has estranged her: nay, I have been *too gentle* with her. I ask you first in candour whether the ambiguity of her behaviour with respect to me, sitting and fondling a man (circumstanced as I was) sometimes for half a day together, and then declaring she had no love for him beyond common regard, and professing never to marry, was not enough to excite my suspicions, which the different exposures from the conversations below-stairs were not calculated to allay? I ask you what you yourself would have felt or done, if loving her as I did, you had heard what I did, time after time? Did not her mother own to one of the grossest charges (which I shall not repeat)—and is such indelicacy to be reconciled with her pretended character (that character with which I fell in love, and to which I *made love*) without supposing her to be the greatest hypocrite in the world? My unpardonable offence has been that I took her at her word, and was willing to believe her the precise little puritanical person she set up for. After exciting her wayward desires by the fondest embraces and the purest kisses, as if she had been 'made my wedded wife yestreen', or was to become so tomorrow (for that was always my feeling with respect to her)—I did not proceed to gratify them, or to follow up my advantage by any action which should declare 'I think you a common adventurer, and will see whether you are so or not!' Yet anyone but a credulous fool like me would have made the experiment, with whatever violence to himself, as a matter of life and death; for I had every reason to distrust appearances. Her conduct has been of a piece from the beginning. In the midst of her closest and falsest endearments, she has always (with one or two exceptions) disclaimed the natural inference to be drawn from them, and made a verbal reservation, by which she might lead me on in a Fool's Paradise, and make me the tool of her levity, her avarice, and her love of intrigue as long as she liked, and dismiss me whenever it suited her. This, you see, she has done, because my intentions grew serious, and if complied with, would deprive her of *the pleasures of a single life!* Offer marriage to this 'tradesman's daughter, who has as nice a sense of honour as anyone can have'; and like Lady Bellaston in *Tom Jones*, she *cuts* you immediately in a fit of abhorrence and alarm. Yet she seemed to be of a different mind formerly, when struggling from me in the height of our first intimacy, she exlaimed 'However I might agree to my own ruin, I never will consent to bring disgrace upon my family!' That I should have spared the traitress after expressions like this astonishes me when I look back upon it. Yet, if it were all to do over again, I know I should act just the same part. Such is her power over me! I cannot run the least risk of offending her—I love her so. When I look in her face, I cannot doubt her truth! Wretched being that I am! I have thrown away my heart and soul upon an unfeeling girl; and my life (that might have been so happy, had she been what I thought her) will soon follow either voluntarily, or by the force of grief, remorse, and disappointment. I cannot get rid of the reflection for an instant, nor even seek relief from its galling pressure. Ah! what a heart she has lost! All the love and affection of my whole life were centered in her, who alone, I thought, of all women had found out my true character, and knew how to value my tenderness. Alas! alas! that this, the only hope, joy, or comfort I ever had, should turn to a mockery, and hang like an ugly film over the remainder of my days!—I was at Roslin Castle yesterday. It lies low in a rude, but sheltered valley, hid from the vulgar gaze, and powerfully reminds one of the old song. The straggling fragments of the russet ruins, suspended smiling and graceful in the air as if they would linger out another century to please the curious beholder, the green larch-trees trembling between with the blue sky and white silver clouds, the wild mountain plants starting out here and there, the date of the year on an old low door-way, but still more, the beds of flowers in orderly decay, that seem to have no hand to tend them, but keep up a sort of traditional remembrance of civilization in former ages, present altogether a delightful and amiable subject for contemplation. The exquisite beauty of the scene, with the thought of what I should feel, should I ever be restored to her, and have to lead her through such places as my adored, my angel-wife, almost drove me beside myself. For this picture, this ecstatic vision, what have I of late instead as the image of the reality? Demoniacal possessions. I see the young witch seated in another's lap, twining her serpent arms round him, her eye glancing and her cheeks on fire—why does not the hideous thought choke me? Or why do I not go and find out the truth at once? The moonlight streams over the silver waters: the bark is in the bay that might waft me to her, almost with a wish. The mountain-breeze sighs out her name: old ocean with a world of tears murmurs back my woes! Does not my heart yearn to be with her; and shall I not follow its bidding? No, I must wait till I am free; and then I will take my Freedom (a glad prize) and lay it at her feet and tell her my proud love of her that would not brook a rival in her dishonour, and that would have her all or none, and gain her or lose myself forever!—

You see by this letter the way I am in, and I hope you will excuse it as the picture of a half-disordered mind. The least respite from my uneasiness (such as I had yesterday) only brings the contrary reflection back upon me, like a flood; and by letting me see the happiness I have lost, makes me feel, by contrast, more acutely what I am doomed to bear.

WILLIAM HAZLITT

Song

Sweetest love, I do not goe,
    For wearinesse of thee,
Nor in hope the world can show
    A fitter Love for mee;
      But since that I
Must dye at last, 'tis best,
To use my selfe in jest
    Thus by fain'd deaths to dye;

Yesternight the Sunne went hence,
    And yet is here to day,
He hath no desire nor sense,
    Nor halfe so short a way:
      Then feare not mee,
But beleeve that I shall make
Speedier journeyes, since I take
    More wings and spurres than hee.

O how feeble is mans power,
    That if good fortune fall,
Cannot adde another houre,
    Nor a lost houre recall!
      But come bad chance,
And wee joyne to'it our strength,
And wee teach it art and length,
    It selfe o'r us to'advance.

When thou sigh'st, thou sigh'st not winde,
    But sigh'st my soule away,
When thou weep'st, unkindly kinde,
    My lifes blood doth decay.
      It cannot bee
That thou lov'st mee, as thou say'st,
If in thine my life thou waste,
    That art the best of mee.

Let not thy divining heart
 Forethinke me any ill,
Destiny may take thy part,
 And may thy feares fulfill;
 But thinke that wee
Are but turn'd aside to sleepe;
They who one another keepe
 Alive, ne'r parted bee.

JOHN DONNE

A Farewell to Arms

The time is World War I: the lovers, an American ambulance driver with the Italian army and an English nurse. She becomes pregnant and they spend the last months of her pregnancy in Switzerland. Catherine's labour goes wrong and after hours of pain and exhaustion she has to have a caesarian. The baby is born dead. This scene begins at the café where Henry has gone to get something to eat.

. . . .

Suddenly I knew I had to get back. I called the waiter, paid the reckoning, got into my coat, put on my hat and started out the door. I walked through the rain up to the hospital.

Upstairs I met the nurse coming down the hall.

'I just called you at the hotel,' she said. Something dropped inside me.

'What is wrong?'

'Mrs Henry has had a haemorrhage.'

'Can I go in?'

'No, not yet. The doctor is with her.'

'Is it dangerous?'

'It is very dangerous.' The nurse went into the room and shut the door. I sat outside in the hall. Everything was gone inside of me. I did not think. I could not think. I knew she was going to die and I prayed that she would not. Don't let her die. Oh, God, please don't let her die. I'll do anything for you if you won't let her die. Please, please, please, dear God, don't let her die. Dear

God, don't let her die. Please, please, please don't let her die. God, please make her not die. You took the baby but don't let her die—that was all right but don't let her die. Please, please, dear God, don't let her die.

The nurse opened the door and motioned with her finger for me to come. I followed her into the room. Catherine did not look up when I came in. I went over to the side of the bed. The doctor was standing by the bed on the opposite side. Catherine looked at me and smiled. I bent down over the bed and started to cry.

'Poor darling,' Catherine said very softly. She looked grey.

'You're all right, Cat,' I said. 'You're going to be all right.'

'I'm going to die,' she said; then waited and said, 'I hate it.'

I took her hand.

'Don't touch me,' she said. I let go of her hand. She smiled. 'Poor darling. You touch me all you want.'

'You'll be all right, Cat. I know you'll be all right.'

'I meant to write you a letter to have if anything happened, but I didn't do it.'

'Do you want me to get a priest or anyone to come and see you.'

'Just you,' she said. Then a little later, 'I'm not afraid. I just hate it.'

'You must not talk so much,' the doctor said.

'All right,' Catherine said.

'Do you want me to do anything, Cat? Can I get you anything?'

Catherine smiled, 'No.' Then a little later, 'You won't do our things with another girl, or say the same things, will you?'

'Never.'

'I want you to have girls, though.'

'I don't want them.'

'You are talking too much,' the doctor said. 'You cannot talk. Mr Henry must go out. He can come back again later. You are not going to die. You must not be silly.'

'All right,' Catherine said. 'I'll come and stay with you nights,' she said. It was very hard for her to talk.

'Please go out of the room' the doctor said. Catherine winked at me, her face grey. 'I'll be right outside,' I said.

'Don't worry, darling,' Catherine said. 'I'm not a bit afraid. It's just a dirty trick.'

'You dear, brave sweet.'

I waited outside in the hall. I waited a long time. The nurse came to the door and came over to me. 'I'm afraid Mrs Henry is very ill,' she said. 'I'm afraid for her.'

'Is she dead?'

'No, but she is unconscious.'

It seems she had one haemorrhage after another. They couldn't stop it. I went into the room and stayed with Catherine until she died. She was unconscious all the time, and it did not take her very long to die.

Outside the room in the hall I spoke to the doctor. 'Is there anything I can do to-night?'

'No. There is nothing to do. Can I take you to your hotel?'

'No, thank you. I am going to stay here a while.'

'I know there is nothing to say. I cannot tell you—'

'No,' I said. 'There's nothing to say.'

'Good night,' he said. 'I cannot take you to your hotel?'

'No, thank you.

'It was the only thing to do,' he said. 'The operation proved—'

'I do not want to talk about it,' I said.

'I would like to take you to your hotel.'

'No, thank you.'

He went down the hall. I went to the door of the room.

'You can't come in now,' one of the nurses said.

'Yes, I can,' I said.

'You can't come in yet.'

'You get out,' I said. 'The other one too.'

But after I had got them out and shut the door and turned off the light it wasn't any good. It was like saying good-bye to a statue. After a while I went out and left the hospital and walked back to the hotel in the rain.

ERNEST HEMINGWAY

The Presence

Why say 'death'? Death is neither harsh nor kind:
Other pleasures or pains could hold the mind
If she were dead. For dead is gone indeed,
Lost beyond recovery and need,
Discarded, ended, rotted underground—
Of whom no personal feature could be found
To stand out from the soft blur evenly spread
On memory, if she were truly dead.

But living still, barred from accustomed use
Of body and dress and motion, with profuse
Reproaches (since this anguish of her grew
Do I still love her as I swear I do?)
She fills the house and garden terribly
With her bewilderment, accusing me,
Till every stone and flower, table and book,
Cries out her name, pierces me with her look,
'You are deaf, listen!
You are blind, see!'
                              How deaf or blind,
When horror of the grave maddens the mind
With those same pangs that lately choked her breath,
Altered her substance, and made sport of death?

ROBERT GRAVES

Part V

OLD LOVE, LAST LOVE, ENDURING LOVE

This is an elusive category: I have included in it a good deal of marriage—happy and otherwise. There is no doubt, for instance, that poor Queen Catherine was not only caused the utmost distress by Henry's defection to Anne Boleyn, she had also to suffer the terrible belief that her beloved husband was doomed to everlasting Hell, added to which she had to leave her plain and sickly only daughter in his doubtful care. In view of all this, her last letter to Henry seems to me filled with the most touching and enduring love. We have Yeats at his best, and Shakespeare at his most majestic; Ursula Vaughan Williams writing about her husband Ralph—a kind of love in safe keeping; a lovely poem by Rochester and 'An Arundel Tomb', one of the best of the always very good indeed Philip Larkin, whose quality, to me, has something in common with Henry Green.

There is John Gay's tender account of Sarah and John, young lovers killed in a hayfield by lightning on the day that her parents had consented to their marriage, and, at the other end of the cycle, Laurie Lee's beautiful epitaph to Hannah and Joseph Brown, married for fifty years and killed by segregation in the workhouse. There is the incomparable scene from *All Quiet on The Western Front* where a whole ward of six men in an army hospital combine to let one badly wounded patient enjoy his wife whom he has not seen for two years. There is also one of the last, if not quite the last, letters that Admiral Collingwood wrote to his wife from whom he was so often and for so long separated, included because it is such a good example of how somebody with no literary pretensions is able, through profound affection, exactly to convey his feelings not only to the recipient, but to any of us reading it now. This last part is chiefly about people who have stayed the course however rough; whose love, returned or not, has endured, and there will always be something striking about that.

Contents

Catharine of Aragon to King Henry VIII (1535)

My Lord and Dear Husband,

I commend me unto you. The hour of my death draweth fast on, and my case being such, the tender love I owe you forceth me, with a few words, to put you in remembrance of the health and safeguard of your soul, which you ought to prefer before all worldly matters, and before the care and tendering of your own body, for the which you have cast me into many miseries and yourself into many cares.

For my part I do pardon you all, yea, I do wish and devoutly pray God that He will also pardon you.

For the rest I commend unto you Mary, our daughter, beseeching you to be a good father unto her, as I heretofore desired. I entreat you also, on behalf of my maids, to give them marriage-portions, which is not much, they being but three. For all my other servants, I solicit a year's pay more than their due, lest they shall be unprovided for,

Lastly, do I vow, that mine eyes desire you
above all things.

Sonnet XLVI

Let me not to the marriage of true minds
   Admit impediments. Love is not love
Which alters when it alteration finds,
   Or bends with the remover to remove.
O, no! it is an ever-fixed mark,
   That looks on tempests and is never shaken;
It is the star to every wandering bark,
   Whose worth's unknown, although his height be taken.
Love's not Times fool, though rosy lips and cheeks
   Within his bending sickle's compass come;
Love alters not with his brief hours and weeks,
   But bears it out even to the edge of doom.
   If this be error, and upon me proved,
   I never writ, nor no man ever loved.

WILLIAM SHAKESPEARE

When You Are Old

When you are old and grey and full of sleep,
And nodding by the fire, take down this book,
And slowly read, and dream of the soft look
Your eyes had once, and of their shadows deep;

How many loved your moments of glad grace,
And loved your beauty with love false or true,
But one man loved the pilgrim soul in you,
And loved the sorrows of your changing face;

And bending down beside the glowing bars,
Murmur, a little sadly, how Love fled
And paced upon the mountains overhead
And hid his face amid a crowd of stars.

W. B. YEATS

All Quiet on the Western Front

The year is 1916, the narrator is twenty; he has been wounded after two years in the trenches and is now recovering in hospital where it has just occurred to him that his 'knowledge of life is limited to death'.

The oldest man in our room is Lewandowski. He is forty, and has already lain ten months in the hospital with a severe abdominal wound. Just in the last few weeks he has improved sufficiently to be able to hobble about doubled up.

For some days past, he has been in great excitement. His wife has written to him from the little home in Poland where she lives, telling him that she has saved up enough money to pay for the fare, and is coming to see him.

She is already on the way and may arrive any day. Lewandowski has lost his appetite, he even gives away red cabbage and sausage after he has had a couple of mouthfuls. He goes round the room perpetually with the letter. Everyone has already read it a dozen times, the post-marks have been examined heaven knows how often, the address is hardly legible any longer for spots of grease and thumb-marks, and in the end what is sure to happen, happens: Lewandowski develops a fever, and has to go back to bed.

He has not seen his wife for two years. In the meantime she has given birth to a child, whom she is bringing with her. But something else occupies Lewandowski's thoughts. He had hoped to get permission to go out when his old woman came; for obviously seeing is all very well, but when a man gets his wife again after such a long time, if at all possible, a man wants something else besides.

Lewandowski has discussed it all with us at great length; in the army there are no secrets about such things. And what's more, nobody finds anything objectionable in it. Those of us who are already able to go out have told him of a couple of very good spots in the town, parks and squares, where he would not be disturbed; one of us even knows of a little room.

But what is the use, there Lewandowski lies in bed with his troubles. Life holds no more joy for him if he has to forego this affair. We console him and promise to get over the difficulty somehow or other.

One afternoon his wife appears, a tousled little thing with anxious, quick eyes like a bird, in a sort of black, crinkly mantilla with ribbons; heaven knows where she inherited the thing.

She murmurs something softly and stands shyly in the doorway. It terrifies her that there are six of us men present.

'Well, Marja,' says Lewandowski, and gulps dangerously with his Adam's apple, 'you can come in all right, they won't hurt you.'

She goes the round and proffers each of us her hand. Then she produces the child, which in the interval has done something in its napkin. From a large handbag embroidered with pearls she takes out a clean one and makes the child fresh and presentable. This dispels her first embarrassment, and the two begin to talk.

Lewandowski is very fidgety, every now and then he squints across at us most unhappily with his round goggle eyes.

The time is favourable, the doctor's visit is over, at the most there couldn't be more than one sister left in the ward. So one of us goes out to prospect. He comes back and nods.

'Not a soul to be seen. Now's your chance, Johann, set to.'

The two speak together in an undertone. The woman turns a little red and looks embarrassed. We grin good-naturedly and make pooh-poohing gestures, what does it matter! The devil take all the conventions, they were made for other times; here lies the carpenter Johann Lewandowski, a soldier shot to a·cripple, and there is his wife; who knows when he will see her again? He wants to have her and he should have her, good.

Two men stand at the door to forestall the sisters and keep them occupied if they chance to come along. They agree to stand guard for a quarter of an hour or thereabouts.

Lewandowski can only lie on his side, so one of us props a couple of pillows against his back. Albert gets the child to hold, we all turn round a bit, the black mantilla disappears under the bed-clothes, we make a great clatter and play skat noisily.

All goes well. I hold a club solo with four jacks which nearly goes the round. In the process we almost forget Lewandowski. After a while the child begins to squall, although Albert, in desperation, rocks it to and fro. Then there is a bit of creaking and rustling, and as we look up casually we see that the child has the bottle in its mouth, and is back again with its mother. The business is over.

We now feel ourselves like one big family, the woman is rather quieter, and Lewandowski lies there sweating and beaming.

He unpacks the embroidered handbag, and a couple of good sausages comes to light; Lewandowski takes up the knife with a flourish and saws the meat into slices.

With a handsome gesture he waves toward us—and the little woman goes from one to the other and smiles at us and hands round the sausage; she now looks quite handsome. We call her Mother, she is pleased and shakes up our pillows for us.

E. M. REMARQUE
translated by A. W. WHEEN

Spoken to a Bronze Head

Bronze, where my curious fingers run
matching each muscle and each metal feature
with life's austerer structure of the bone,
each living plane and contour so well known,
you will endure beyond the span of nature,
be as you are now when our lives are done.

On unborn generations you will stare
with the same hollow eyes I touch and see,
look on a world in which no memories share
the living likeness of the face you wear,
keep, in unchanged serenity
all that time gave him in your guardian care.

His name is yours to keep, so will his glory be,
who are his only, his inheriting son:
and when the hand that writes so ardently
the sound of unknown sound reaches finality,
the music captured, all the work well done,
stand in his place and bravely wear his immortality.

URSULA VAUGHAN WILLIAMS

To Lady Collingwood

Cherished Hopes of returning to his Family.

Ocean, June 16, 1806.

This day, my love, is the anniversary of our marriage, and I
wish you many happy returns of it. If ever we have peace, I hope
to spend my latter days amid my family, which is the only sort of
happiness I can enjoy. After this life of labour to retire to peace
and quietness is all I look for in the world. Should we decide to
change the place of our dwelling, our route would of course be to
the southward of Morpeth; but then I should be for ever regret-

ting those beautiful views which are nowhere to be exceeded; and even the rattling of that old waggon that used to pass our door at six o'clock in a winter's morning had its charms. The fact is, whenever I think how I am to be happy again, my thoughts carry me back to Morpeth, where, out of the fuss and parade of the world, surrounded by those I loved most dearly, and who loved me, I enjoyed as much happiness as my nature is capable of. Many things that I see in the world give me a distaste to the finery of it. The great knaves are not like those poor unfortunates, who, driven perhaps to distress from accidents which they could not prevent, or at least not educated in principles of honour and honesty, are hanged for some little thievery; while a knave of education and high-breeding, who brandishes his honour in the eyes of the world, would rob a state to its ruin. For the first I feel pity and compassion; for the latter, abhorrence and contempt; they are the tenfold vicious.

Have you read—but what I am more interested about, is your sister with you, and is she well and happy? Tell her—God bless her!—I wish I were with you, that we might have a good laugh. God bless me! I have scarcely laughed these three years. I am here with a very reduced force, having been obliged to make detachments to all quarters. This leaves me weak, while the Spaniards and French within are daily gaining strength. They have patched and pieced until they have now a very considerable fleet. Whether they will venture out, I do not know; if they come, I have no doubt we shall do an excellent deed, and then I will bring them to England myself.

How do the dear girls go on? I would have them taught geometry, which is of all sciences in the world the most entertaining; it expands the mind more to the knowledge of all things in nature, and better teaches to distinguish between truths and such things as have the appearance of being truths, yet are not, than any other. Their education, and the proper cultivation of the sense which God has given them, are the objects on which my happiness most depends. To inspire them with a love of everything that is honourable and virtuous, though in rags, and with contempt for vanity in embroidery, is the way to make them the darlings of my heart. They should not only read, but it requires a careful selection of books; nor should they ever have access to two at the same time; but when a subject is begun, it should be finished before anything else is undertaken. How would it enlarge their minds if they could acquire a sufficient knowledge of mathematics and astronomy to give them an idea of the beauty and wonders of the creation! I am persuaded that the generality of people, and particularly fine ladies, only adore God because they are told it is proper, and the fashion to go to church; but I would have my girls gain such knowledge of the works of the creation, that they may have a fixed idea of the nature of that Being who could be the author of such a world. Whenever they have that, nothing on this side the moon will give them much uneasiness of mind. I do not mean that they should be stoics, or want the common feelings for the sufferings that flesh is heir to; but they would then have a source of consolation for the worst that could happen.

Tell me how do the trees which I planted thrive? Is there shade under the three oaks for a comfortable summer-seat? Do the poplars grow at the walk, and does the wall of the terrace stand firm? My bankers tell me that all my money in their hands is exhausted by fees on the peerage, and that I am in their debt, which is a new epoch in my life, for it is the first time I was ever in debt since I was a midshipman. Here I got nothing; but then my expenses are nothing, and I do not want it particularly, now that I have got my knives, forks, tea-pot, and the things you were so kind as to send me.

ADMIRAL LORD COLLINGWOOD

A Young Lady to Her Ancient Lover

This 'Song of a Young Lady to her Ancient Lover' is in fact not by a young lady, but by John Wilmot, Earl of Rochester.

Ancient Person, for whom I
All the flattering Youth defy:
Long be it ere thou grow Old,
Aching, shaking, crazy Cold.
But still continue as thou art,
Ancient Person of my Heart.

On thy wither'd Lips and Dry
Which like barren Furrows lye,
Brooding Kisses I will pour
Shall thy Youthful Heat restore.
Such kind show'rs in Autumn fall,
And a Second Spring recall:
Nor from thee will ever part,
Ancient Person of my Heart.

Thy Nobler parts which but to name
In our Sex would be counted shame,
By Age's frozen grasp possest,
From their ice shall be releast:
And sooth'd by my reviving hand
In former warmth and vigour stand.
All a lover's wish can reach
For thy Joy my love shall teach.
And for thy Pleasure shall improve
All that Art can add to Love.
Yes still I love thee without Art,
Ancient Person of my Heart.

Cider With Rosie

This is the author's recollection of an old couple who lived near his village in Gloucestershire.

But if you survived melancholia and rotting lungs it was possible to live long in this valley. Joseph and Hannah Brown, for instance, appeared to be indestructible. For as long as I could remember they had lived together in the same house up by the common. They had lived there, it was said, for fifty years; which seemed to me for ever. They had raised a large family and sent them into the world, and had continued to live on alone, with nothing left of their noisy brood save some dog-eared letters and photographs.

The old couple were as absorbed in themselves as lovers, content and self-contained; they never left the village or each other's company, they lived as snug as two podded chestnuts. By day blue smoke curled up from their chimney, at night the red windows glowed; the cottage, when we passed it, said 'Here live the Browns', as though that were part of nature.

Though white and withered, they were active enough, but they ordered their lives without haste. The old woman cooked, and threw grain to the chickens, and hung out her washing on bushes; the old man fetched wood and chopped it with a billhook, did a bit of gardening now and then, or just sat on a seat outside his door and gazed at the valley, or slept. When summer came they bottled fruit, and when winter came they ate it. They did nothing more than was necessary to live, but did it fondly, with skill— then sat together in their clock-ticking kitchen enjoying their half-century of silence. Whoever called to see them was welcomed gravely, be it man or beast or child; and to me they resembled two tawny insects, slow but deft in their movements; a little foraging, some frugal feeding, then any amount of stillness. They spoke to each other without raised voices, in short chirrups as brief as bird-song, and when they moved about in their tiny kitchen they did so smoothly and blind, gliding on worn, familiar rails, never bumping or obstructing each other. They were fond, pink-faced, and alike as cherries, having taken and merged, through their years together, each other's looks and accents.

It seemed that the old Browns belonged for ever, and that the miracle of their survival was made commonplace by the durability of their love—if one should call it love, such a balance. Then suddenly, within the space of two days, feebleness took them both. It was as though two machines, wound up and synchronized, had run down at exactly the same time. Their interdependence was so legendary we didn't notice their plight at first. But after a week, not having been seen about, some neighbours thought it best to call. They found old Hannah on the kitchen floor feeding her man with a spoon. He was lying in a corner half-covered with matting, and they were both too weak to stand. She had chopped up a plate of peelings, she said, as she hadn't been able to manage the fire. But they were all right really, just a touch of the damp; they'd do, and it didn't matter.

Well, the Authorities were told, the Visiting Spinsters got busy; and it was decided they would have to be moved. They were too frail to help each other now, and their children were too scattered, oo busy. There was but one thing to be done; it was for the best; they would have to be moved to the Workhouse.

The old couple were shocked and terrified, and lay clutching each others hands. 'The Workhouse'—always a word of shame, grey shadow falling on the close of life, most feared by the old (even when called The Infirmary); abhorred more than debt, or prison, or beggary, or even the stain of madness.

Hannah and Joseph thanked the Visiting Spinsters but pleaded to be left at home, to be left as they wanted, to cause no trouble, just simply to stay together. The Workhouse could not give them the mercy they needed, but could only divide them in charity. Much better to hide, or die in a ditch, or to starve in one's familiar kitchen, watched by the objects one's life had gathered—the scrubbed empty table, the plates and saucepans, the cold grate, the white stopped clock. . . .

'You'll be well looked after,' the Spinsters said, 'and you'll see each other twice a week.' The bright busy voices cajoled with authority and the old couple were not trained to defy them. So that same afternoon, white and speechless, they were taken away to the Workhouse. Hannah Brown was put to bed in the Woman's Wing, and Joseph lay in the Men's. It was the first time, in all their fifty years, that they had ever been separated. They did not see each other again, for in a week they both were dead.

I was haunted by their end as by no other, and by the kind, killing Authority that arranged it. Divided, their life went out of them, so they ceased as by mutual agreement. Their cottage stood empty on the edge of the common, its front door locked and soundless. Its stones grew rapidly cold and repellent with its life so suddenly withdrawn. In a year it fell down, first the roof, then the walls, and lay scattered in a tangle of briars. Its decay was so violent and overwhelming, it was as though the old couple had wrecked it themselves.

Soon all that remained of Joe and Hannah Brown, and of their long close life together, were some grass-grown stumps, a garden gone wild, some rusty pots, and a dog-rose.

LAURIE LEE

John Anderson my Jo
(from The Scots Musical Museum, 1790)

John Anderson my jo, John,
   When we were first acquent,
Your locks were like the raven,
   Your bonnie brow was brent;
But now your brow is beld, John,
   Your locks are like the snow;
But blessings on your frosty pow,
   John Anderson, my jo.

John Anderson my jo, John,
   We clamb the hill thegither;
And mony a canty day, John,
   We've had wi' ane anither:
Now we maun totter down, John,
   And hand in hand we'll go,
And sleep thegither at the foot,
   John Anderson, my jo.

William Pitt to his Wife, Lady Chatham

February 22, 1766 (past 4 o'clock).
Happy, indeed, was the scene of this glorious morning (for at past one we divided), when the sun of liberty shone once more benignly upon a country too long benighted. My dear love, not all the applauding joy which the hearts of animated gratitude, saved from despair and bankruptcy, uttered in the lobby, could touch me, in any degree, like the tender and lively delight which breathes in your warm and affectionate note.

All together, my dearest life, makes me not ill to-day after the immense fatigue, or not feeling that I am so. Wonder not if I should find myself in a placid and sober fever, for tumultuous exultation you know I think not permitted to feeble mortal successes; but my delight, heartfelt and solid as it is, must want its sweetest ingredient (if not its very essence) till I rejoice with my angel, and with her join in thanksgivings to protecting Heaven for all our happy deliverances.

Thank you for the sight of Smith; his honest joy and affection charm me. Loves to the sweet babes, patriotic or not; though I hope *impetuous William* is not behind in feelings of that kind. Send the saddle-horses if you please, so as to be in town early to-morrow morning. I propose and hope to execute my journey to Hayes by eleven.

Your ever loving husband,
W. PITT.

Memoir

I have just passed part of this summer at an old romantic seat of my Lord Harcourt's which he lent me. It overlooks a common hayfield, where, under the shade of a haycock, sat two lovers—as constant as ever were found in romance—beneath a spreading bush. The name of the one (let it sound as it will) was John Hewet; of the other Sarah Drew. John was a well-set man, about five-and-twenty; Sarah, a brave woman of eighteen. John had for several months borne the labour of the day in the same field with Sarah; when she milked, it was his morning and evening charge to bring the cows to her pails. Their love was the talk, but not the scandal, of the whole neighbourhood, for all they aimed at was the blameless possession of each other in marriage. It was but this very morning he had obtained her parents' consent, and it was but till the next week that they were to wait to be happy. While they were thus employed (it was on the last of July), a terrible storm of thunder and lightning arose, that drove the labourers to what shelter the trees or hedges afforded. Sarah, frightened and out of breath, sunk on a haycock; and John (who never separated from her) sat by her side, having raked two or three heaps together, to secure her. Immediately, there was heard so loud a crash, as if heaven had burst asunder. The labourers, all solicitous for each other's safety called to one another: those that were nearest our lovers, hearing no answer, stepped to the place where they lay: they first saw a little smoke, and, after, this faithful pair—John, with one arm about his Sarah's neck, and the other held over her face, as if to screen her from the lightning. They were struck dead, and already grown stiff and cold in this tender posture. There was no mark or discolouring on their bodies—only that Sarah's eyebrow was a little singed, and a small spot between her breasts. They were buried the next day in one grave.

JOHN GAY

The Chastity of Married Life
(from Le Jardin Secret)

Even when couples remain, as people say, in love with each other, their love is of a peaceful and patient kind. This unexpected thing happens, which one would not believe if one had not experienced it—the presence of the accustomed companion at one's side becomes in the end an element of physical calm. Husbands do not, as a rule, care to confess it, and the wives who complain of being deserted are rare—most of us would find a renewal of our husbands' advances rather disagreeable. But nothing is more chaste, in reality, than the majority of households; nothing in them evokes passion. Passion depends upon uncertainty and brevity in regard to time; while the hours of a married couple are inordinately long and regular.

MARCEL PRÉVOST

An Arundel Tomb

Side by side, their faces blurred,
The earl and countess lie in stone,
Their proper habits vaguely shown
As jointed armour, stiffened pleat,
And that faint hint of the absurd—
The little dogs under their feet.

Such plainness of the pre-baroque
Hardly involves the eye, until
It meets his left-hand gauntlet, still
Clasped empty in the other; and
One sees, with a sharp tender shock,
His hand withdrawn, holding her hand.

They would not think to lie so long.
Such faithfulness in effigy
Was just a detail friends would see:
A sculptor's sweet commissioned grace
Thrown off in helping to prolong
The Latin names around the base.

They would not guess how early in
Their supine stationary voyage
The air would change to soundless damage,
Turn the old tenantry away;
How soon succeeding eyes begin
To look, not read. Rigidly they

Persisted, linked, through lengths and breadths
Of time. Snow fell, undated. Light
Each summer thronged the glass. A bright
Litter of birdcalls strewed the same
Bone-riddled ground. And up the paths
The endless altered people came,

Washing at their identity.
Now, helpless in the hollow of
An unarmorial age, a trough
Of smoke in slow suspended skeins
Above their scrap of history,
Only an attitude remains:

Time has transfigured them into
Untruth. The stone fidelity
They hardly meant has come to be
Their final blazon, and to prove
Our almost-instinct almost true:
What will survive of us is love.

PHILIP LARKIN

ACKNOWLEDGEMENTS

The editor and the publishers wish to thank the following for permission to use copyright material in this anthology:

'Love an Escape from Loneliness', from *Marriage and Morals*, Bertrand Russell, George Allen & Unwin Ltd

All Quiet on the Western Front, Erich Maria Remarque, reprinted by permission of Putnam & Co

Tender is the Night, from *Scott Fitzgerald Volume II*, The Bodley Head

Something in Disguise, Elizabeth Jane Howard, Jonathan Cape Ltd

My Young Years, Arthur Rubinstein, Jonathan Cape Ltd

'Green Heart', from *A Look Round the Estate*, Kingsley Amis, Jonathan Cape Ltd

'Jig', 'Hornpipe' and 'Sonnet', from *Collected Poems*, 1954, C. Day Lewis, the Executors of the Estate of C. Day Lewis, The Hogarth Press, Jonathan Cape Ltd

'The Mirror', from *Pegasus and Other Poems*, C. Day Lewis, the Executors of the Estate of C. Day Lewis, Jonathan Cape Ltd

'In the Orchard', from *Selected Poems*, Muriel Stuart, the Executors of the Muriel Stuart Estate, Jonathan Cape Ltd

A Farewell to Arms, Ernest Hemingway, the Executors of the Ernest Hemingway Estate, Jonathan Cape Ltd

The Young Visiters, Daisy Ashford, Chatto & Windus Ltd

First Love, Ivan Turgenev, translation Isaiah Berlin, Curtis Brown Ltd

A Game of Hide and Seek, Elizabeth Taylor, Estate of the late Elizabeth Taylor and Peter Davies (Publishers)

'An Arundel Tomb', from *The Whitsun Weddings*, Philip Larkin, Faber & Faber Ltd

INDEX OF AUTHORS